LIFE CHOICES
Applying Sociology

LIFE CHOICES
Applying Sociology

ROBERT E. KENNEDY, JR.
University of Minnesota, Minneapolis, Minnesota

HOLT, RINEHART AND WINSTON
New York   Chicago   San Francisco   Philadelphia
Montreal   Toronto   London   Sydney
Tokyo   Mexico City   Rio de Janeiro   Madrid

Ira L. Reiss, "Some Observations on Ideology and Sexuality in America," *Journal of Marriage and the Family* (May, 1981), Vol. 43, No. 2, pages 273–281. Copyrighted 1981 by the National Council of Family Relations, Fairview Community School Center, 1910 West County Road B, Suite 147, St. Paul, MN 55113. Quoted and paraphrased by permission.

Library of Congress Cataloging in Publication Data

Kennedy, Robert E., 1937–
  Life choices.

  Bibliography: p.
  Includes index.
  1. Sociology. 2. Choice (Psychology) 3. Decision-making. 4. Social choice. 5. Social values. I. Title.
HM73.K46 1986   301   85-7652

ISBN 0-03-069634-8

CBS COLLEGE PUBLISHING
Holt, Rinehart and Winston
The Dryden Press
Saunders College Publishing

Acknowledgments

Many people made this book possible. My parents, wife, and son provided much-needed support and encouragement, and also made major contributions to the book's content and writing style.

I am grateful to the following people for their thoughtful reviews of the manuscript and their helpful suggestions: Jan Fritz, Georgetown University; James H. Gundlach, Auburn University; Carla Howery; Donald P. Irish, Hamline University; Toshimasa Kii, Georgia State University; Betty Frankle Kirschner, Kent State University; Edward C. Knop, Colorado State University; Ed Lanctot; Anne Martin, Edmonds Community College; Reece J. McGee, Purdue University; Richard C. Stanville, Normandale Community College; Margaret Brooks Terry, Baldwin-Wallace College; and my colleagues and associates at the University of Minnesota—Ramona Asher, Gloria DeWolfe, Jan Fiola, Lucy Rose Fischer, Katherine Simon Frank, Jeylan T. Mortimer, and Margaret Roden.

The book materialized and took final form through the creative energy and careful management of Marie Schappert and Earl McPeek, Acquisitions Editors, Susan Hajjar, Developmental Editor, and the staff at Holt, Rinehart and Winston.

Contents

Tables

Figures and Questionnaires

FIGURE

QUESTIONNAIRE

LIFE CHOICES
Applying Sociology

Introduction

Since I began teaching sociology in the late 1960s, I have been impressed by the number of college students who take sociology courses to learn more about life. Many want to know how social systems work, how cultural values affect personal choices, and how life prospects are influenced by social forces. The best way I found to meet this student interest was to highlight the age-related aspects of a sociological topic. The focus on age fits in naturally with the life-course perspective, making an easily understood and intriguing combination. Because a brief and clearly written book taking this approach did not exist, I decided to fill that gap.

I hope *Life Choices* will help readers improve their life prospects by showing them how to apply sociological knowledge to their own lives. The book does this in three ways. First, it provides factual information showing how personal decisions are made in a social context. Second, using simple questionnaires, the book asks readers to reflect on the values in which they believe and, by so doing, to consider how important cultural values are in making personal decisions. And third, it uses population projections to show some life situations that can be reasonably expected in the future. On this last point, no attempt is made to forecast what will happen—that is unknowable. Instead, the projections are intended to encourage taking a long-term view about possible consequences of one's decisions.

Given the emphasis on making personal choices, and my desire for a concise book, I wrote it for a specific audience—undergraduate college students from first-term freshmen through seniors, including students who are beyond the customary ages of most college undergraduates. For many people, higher education opens a wider range of opportunities, increases their freedom to make choices, and enhances awareness of the consequences of their decisions. Thus, many of the topics included, and examples used, were selected to show college-educated people the difference that having a college education makes in their lives.

I would have liked to include detailed discussions about the life choices of people who do not go to college. There is no lack of information about their lives. Such statistics are listed in many of the same sources that I use to describe the lives of people with some college education. If I had added an equal amount of material about the noncollege population, however, it would have hampered a straightforward treatment of the college-educated population's life choices and prospects. The book also would have been much longer, and the added pages would have increased its cost to students.

Similarly, my striving for a concise book meant minimizing the duplication of materials commonly included in most sociology textbooks. I would have liked to elaborate on many social patterns described in this book, especially the causes and consequences of class, racial, and gender inequities. But I did not do so because that information is readily available in many standard texts.

Life Choices is not a substitute for a comprehensive sociology text, or a course instructor's own lectures and materials. Instead, it can serve as a supplement to both. It can be read straight through either at the start or near the end of a course, or chapters can be assigned to be read with related chapters in a main text. *Life Choices* chapters are linked to general topics in many sociology textbooks in the following way:

LIFE CHOICES Chapter	*Main Text Topic*
1. Thinking about Your Future	What Is Sociology? Population, Life Course
2. Life Prospects and Cohort Size	Research Methods, Population, Social Change
3. How Much Formal Education?	Education, Social Statification, Gender Relations, Race Relations
4. Which Occupation?	Work and Occupations, Gender Relations, Social Change
5. Married or Unmarried?	Family, Sexuality, Gender Relations
6. Childfree or Parent?	Family, Social Change
7. Homeowner or Renter? Mover or Stayer?	Community Life, Urban Life, Social Stratification, Migration, Race Relations, Social Change
8. What Can You Expect in Retirement?	Aging, Population, Social Change, Gender Relations
9. Making Choices in an Age of Uncertainty	Life Course, Social Change, Aging

Life Choices can be especially useful to students in introductory classes where the main text attempts an overview of the entire field of sociology. Too often students perceive such a text as overwhelming, giving them answers without first making clear what the questions are. In contrast, most chapters in this book ask specific questions before providing detailed and factual answers. Having seen in this book how the sociological perspective can give clear answers to a limited number of important questions, readers may be encouraged to apply the same approach to other matters, including decisions made on the job and as citizens.

The purpose of the questionnaires included in this book is simply to help readers make plain their preferences for certain occupations, being married or single, having children or not, and so forth. For the sake of clarity, each questionnaire groups similar values and labels them. While this approach points up which values are connected with what choices, it does involve an unavoidable tradeoff—answers may be influenced by the fact that value items have been grouped and categorized.

Course instructors can improve the validity of student responses to the value questions, however, by constructing one questionnaire that mixes together all of the items in the different chapters. By administering that combined questionnaire on the first day of class, instructors can provide students with both their individual results, and the class total for each item. If desired, the questionnaire can be readministered near the end of the course. Any differences from the first-day responses can be discussed in light of what students have learned so far in sociology. Debates over conflicting values and ideas can help students (and sociologists) test their theories against reality.

A final word about my own values. . . . Given the emphasis throughout the book on the importance of individual choice in life, it should be apparent that I see people as shapers—and not victims—of society. Certainly, our lives are constrained by social forces. Culture and socialization do limit our goals, preferences, and opinions. Social structure can restrict our alternatives. The narrowing of options gradually imposed on us by the aging process, for example, is a major theme of this book. Another theme, the importance of population processes for our life prospects, also reveals how personal choices are constrained by matters beyond our control.

Nevertheless, in a rapidly changing and fluid society such as the United States, I believe that uncertainty about the future is as common a problem as people having too little freedom to make their own decisions. People in their late teens and early twenties, for example, have a wider range of possible futures, and more uncertainty, than they probably will have thirty or forty years later. Thus, it is particularly important, I believe, for young adults to combine the sociological perspective with sound knowledge of the society in which they live, to judge their own life prospects and make their own life choices.

1 /

Thinking about Your Future

You are unique in your personality, capabilities, desires, and experiences. But no one is an island—we all live in social settings. As you go through your life, many problems and opportunities you face as an individual will be similar, though not identical, to those facing thousands, if not millions, of other people your age. You will be sharing your life with your agemates, and their numbers will influence your life chances. This book will use projections of your agemates' prospects to take you on a journey through some major choices you may make during your life, including those about education, occupation, marriage, rearing children, housing, and retirement.

No attempt is made in this book to forecast what will happen either to you or to society at large. Your life will be different from anyone else's. You probably will experience unexpected events, both good and bad. And if you also believe, as I do, that large-scale social, economic, and political events, nationally and internationally, have major consequences for your individual life, then forecasting becomes even more difficult. The farther into the future that predictions of national and international events are made, the less reliable they become. A "long-term" forecast of inflation or unemployment rates may cover only the next six months, while your remaining lifetime could well be more than sixty years.

Even though you cannot predict your future in detail, you can reduce the harmful impact of unexpected events on your life. My basic assumption is that you can better control your life if you understand life events most people experience. You can anticipate some life situations by learning from others who already have been there. You also can ask yourself what may happen to you if certain trends or events materialize. In both cases you are thinking about your future life choices. Your goal is not simply to worry about the future but to improve your life prospects. To act rationally you need to know what to expect.

The purpose of this book is to increase your knowledge of events, options, and choices during your life. By adding useful ideas and knowledge to the intellectual toolbox you carry with you throughout your life, you will be able to transform some unexpected crises into anticipated transitions, and perhaps avoid making some major mistakes.

A SOCIOLOGICAL VIEW OF LIFE

You may sometimes feel that your life is determined too much by the expectations of other people—that you are not leading your life but simply acting out roles already written for you by your parents, friends, teachers or employers, and others. You are taking a sociological view of your life when you feel this way. You are realizing how important social pressures are to you.

Most people go along with the expectations placed on them because they realize they depend on others for what they want in life. But they don't have to. They can free themselves from a particular expectation if they give up the rewards of acting in an expected manner and accept the penalties.

Some people claim they have little or no choice, that society and social pressures entirely determine their lives. But they are mistaken. They are accepting what sociologist Dennis H. Wrong calls an "oversocialized view of man," and are not giving sufficient weight to individual differences in health, abilities, and emotional makeup. They have a choice, and so do you.

Your power of choice means that while "society" or some mix of "social forces" may constrain your options, they do not entirely determine your life. Social patterns exist; life is not random. Discrimination by age, sex, and race does exist, but not all whites succeed, and not all blacks fail. What the individual chooses to do at certain turning points in life can make a difference—personal actions have consequences. Opportunities can be exploited or squandered; difficulties can be overcome or compounded.

Social pressures are a part of living. How well you deal with them will influence how well you will succeed in handling your life. As sociologist C. Wright Mills emphasized, the first benefits of a sociological view of life are realizations that: (1) you can anticipate your life chances only by learning about other persons in your circumstances; and (2) you can gauge your future only by locating yourself in historical time. To handle social pressures well, you must know something about the major social forces around you—values, social institutions, and society-wide processes.

Major Social Forces

When you willingly conform to the expectations of others, you do so because of values in which you have chosen to believe. In the United States, for example, many widely held values concern material success. One such social value assumes there is a connection between personal worthiness and the accumulation of material wealth. If you accept this value, you may think it is human nature. But it is not, because it is not found in every society.

Values are principles for thought and action that you share in common with others in the society. Values are the standards by which goals are chosen, and not the goals themselves. Linking personal worthiness with material wealth is a social value. Making a million dollars before turning forty is a specific goal.

The values you believe in may or may not be compatible with your individual psychological needs or motives. You may value the conspicuous consumption of goods yet feel shy about doing what is needed to earn a high income. You may turn down an opportunity to earn a high income as a salesperson working only for commissions, for example, because the job requires you to deal with strangers. You may value security and physical safety, yet feel bored leading a cautious life centered around avoiding risk. In spite of valuing job security, you may quit a government postal clerk job, for example, simply because you find the work uninteresting.

Based on your values, you expect others to act in certain ways. They will if they share your values. Such shared values lead to mutual expectations of what constitutes appropriate behavior. Mutual expectations held by large groups of people create social institutions, and the various institutions are each concerned with certain aspects of life. Family institutions, for example, are concerned with expected behavior dealing with such things as sexual relationships and the care of dependent children. Economic institutions involve making a living, distributing material wealth, and dealing with poverty. Through educational institutions useful skills are taught and cultural philosophies are transferred.

As a member of various groups, you share in your groups' fortunes even though they may be caused by events and processes over which you, as an individual, have little or no control. Such events and processes include—but are not limited to—inflation; unemployment; population growth; international trade patterns; military buildups; environmental change; the spread of mass education; and the widespread use of satellite communications, computers, and robots.

You may have no detailed knowledge of these seemingly abstract and distant matters, but they influence your life nevertheless. Shared values, social institutions through which values are implemented, and the underlying society-wide processes all directly shape your available personal choices throughout your life course. This idea can be expressed graphically:

Starting Point

Ending Point

Shared Values   →   Social   →   Societal   →   Possible
                 Institutions   Processes   Personal
                                                            Actions

Becoming Self-Directing

In many traditional societies, or in a modern religious cult, only one set of values is tolerated, social control is rigidly enforced by effective social institutions, and underlying societal processes change slowly. Under these conditions, individuals have little liberty in making their life choices. But the situation is different in our American society today. In many aspects of everyday life, several alternative sets of values are tolerated. Social institutions are flexible and at times ineffective in controlling individual behavior. Social and technological change is rapid. Individuals have a great deal of freedom in making their life choices.

It is not surprising that many do not know what is expected of them and are puzzled about what to do. They may not hold firm values. They may not receive clear guidance from their social institutions. Nevertheless, the impersonal societal processes continue and, by default, become the determining influences on personal actions. The result is that the individual is buffeted by large-scale social, political, and economic forces as is a ship without a rudder.

How can you avoid such a turn of events? The answer lies in first becoming aware of the power you have to make your own life choices and to take responsibility for yourself. The opportunity to be self-directing depends on your prior choices, the knowledge you have gained, and the credentials you have earned. As sociologist David Riesman argued in his classic book, *The Lonely Crowd*, a case can be made for becoming self-directing (autonomous) in leading your life, instead of being either tradition-, inner-, or other-directed.

Tradition-directed persons try to lead their lives as their parents and grandparents before them did, an approach poorly suited to rapidly changing conditions. Inner-directed persons adopt strongly held values early in life, rarely alter them, and use changing opportunities to achieve their goals as best they can. They can cope with economic and technological change more successfully than tradition-directed persons. The single-minded pursuit of inner-directed persons toward their goals can even accelerate the pace of social change. But inner-directed persons have difficulty adjusting to shifts in cultural values. They can find themselves holding values no longer shared by others and pursuing goals no longer attainable under current conditions.

Other-directed persons have no fixed values or goals. They are flexible in their beliefs, responding more to what is currently fashionable among their friends than to traditional values or to their childhood training. They are acutely sensitive to the ever-changing criteria and expectations presented by television, radio, motion pictures, and magazines. The ease with which they adapt permits them to keep up with rapid technological, social, and cultural change. Without traditional values, or strongly held personal values, however, other-directed persons have difficulty taking a long-range view of their lives. Their decisions and commitments often are too short term and too dependent on what may become fashionable next year. Decisions made on the basis of short-term considerations alone may turn out to be mistakes in the long run.

Autonomous persons differ from the other three by combining the commitment to thinking for themselves of the inner-directed with the willingness to change of the other-directed. They take a long-range view and hold their chosen values firmly regardless of passing fashions or social pressures. But they also recognize that their personal situations may change, and that large-scale social processes can affect their lives. They are willing to leave some values behind and accept new ones.

If you wish to become more self-directing, you should ask yourself this question: are some basic values I have adopted as human nature instead social standards that I can now choose to accept or reject? I have argued, for example, that the pursuit of ever-increasing material wealth is not a universal human trait because it is behavior found only among some people in some societies. Occupational choice is another example of a value-based decision. In the United States almost all men and most women participate in the labor force at some time during their lives. But what criteria will you use in selecting your particular occupation? Will it be the pursuit of individual success no matter who stands in your way? Or will it be giving service at low pay to persons in need? Or will it be still another set of values? You may think that marriage and parenthood are human nature. Almost everyone eventually marries, and most people have children. But some do not marry, and some married people do not have children.

What course will you take? In answering such questions, what values (standards for deciding actions and attitudes) should you use? If you have no firm values, you have no basis for making consistent choices about important life decisions. Whatever you do, the fact remains that it is your choice and not society's.

Your Life's Social Context

Having chosen to believe in certain social values, then do you also accept the social pressures that accompany the values? If you believe, for example, that one should not marry until one can support a family, then are you willing to resist social pressures to marry before finishing your formal education?

Because social pressures often are felt in intensely personal circumstances, it helps to step out of yourself and view your situation objectively.

You may ask yourself such questions as: what were the consequences for those who married early (or late) judged by the values that I hold? Were any of these consequences due to conditions that existed in the past but which may be different when I arrive at that stage in my life? For example, which occupations are dying, which are growing? Will the job market five years from now require a higher level of formal education for the occupation I seek than it did five years ago?

Your goal is to view your life in its social context. After informing yourself about these matters, you may make the same choices as you would have made originally. But your decisions will have been made with greater realism, confidence, and commitment, and will be less a matter of social pressure or mere chance. You will be using the sociological perspective to improve your ability to think for yourself.

A long-term view is necessary for this approach because choices you make at one stage in life directly influence your later options. And you may live longer than you think. Among people in their late teens in 1985, the Social Security Administration is projecting that nine of ten women and three of four men will live into their early seventies. Surprisingly large minorities will go on to celebrate birthdays in their early nineties: over one-third of the women and one-seventh of the men.

The choice of whether to have children illustrates the long-lasting effect of early life choices. People who live into their late eighties who had chosen fifty or more years earlier not to have or adopt any children will have no sons or daughters, grandsons or granddaughters to turn to in case of need in the final decades of their lives. Whatever good reasons they had for remaining childless, their thinking should have taken into account the future lack of family resources. Long before they become aged, childless persons should provide other sources of social and financial support for themselves.

The emphasis in this book is on showing you the process of thinking about your own life course from a long-term, sociological perspective. You may share my belief that personal benefits flow from living your life with an eye to the future. If so, I hope the excitement of discovering things about your own life course will encourage you to continue to use this intellectual skill throughout your life. You may want to keep this book and refer to it when you reach those events in your life that are now some years distant. The organization of the book will continue to provide a useful framework for thinking about certain life choices. The range of options available to you later may be much the same as they are to people who are facing the same events in their lives today.

SOME USEFUL DEMOGRAPHIC IDEAS

Having selected values from your upbringing, education, readings, experiences, and associations, and having accepted the corresponding expectations of the related social institutions, you still must deal with large-scale social, political, and economic processes. A rational question you may want to continually ask yourself is: how may my own personal life chances be altered by national or international forces beyond my control over, say, the next twenty years? You are not seeking complete knowledge. That would be an unending task. Instead the goal is to keep an open mind about how major societal changes may affect your own life. You want to keep informed about how your personal choices may be influenced by an ever-changing flux of opportunities and constraints.

Population Projections

I have found that this seemingly overwhelming task becomes much more manageable when organized around population projections. The number of people you may share your life with is a good starting point for talking about your life prospects. Many of your life choices will be influenced by the sheer number of other people wanting the same things you may want, including education, jobs, housing, energy, food, clean air and water, protection from crime, and security in old age.

Unlike some social processes, population trends are more easily understood because they result from only three factors—births, deaths, and people moving from one place to another. One can project how large a population may become by making calculations based on clearly stated assumptions about each of these three factors. When population projections are also made by age and sex, then you not only know the number of people with whom you may be sharing your future, but also you know how many there may be that are your own age and sex, and older or younger than you.

Projections are "what if" calculations. They do not attempt to forecast what actually will happen (I believe the future is unknowable in detail), but only what may happen if certain conditions materialize. This book uses government population projections based on "what if" assumptions through the year 2060 to show the options you may have if certain demographic and social trends continue.

Birth Cohorts

By becoming sophisticated in understanding and using population projections, you are adding some beneficial ideas from the demographic perspective to your intellectual toolbox. Demography is the study of human populations—their size, growth, distribution, and composition. The following chapter covers the demographic perspective in more detail, especially the matter of population projections. But for now, consider this unavoidable fact of life: your birthday is not your own. You share it with thousands of other people who were born on the same day. The concept of a birth cohort (all persons born during the same period) is a powerful idea. Your own birth cohort is the link between you, your life course, your place in history, and society.

The idea of birth cohorts allows you to project when you may be experiencing what event in your life. Your age at various times in the future is fixed by your birth date. All you have to do is to live that long. Life-course events are more flexible in their timing—you may be early or late in experiencing some. The more highly age-related the event is, however, the more likely you will experience it at a particular age and thus at a particular time. After helping you locate your life events in time, this book will then briefly describe the important choices open to you, and what sociological and demographic research has shown to be the advantages and disadvantages of the various options you have before you.

Your cohort is your direct connection with the larger society because millions of other people were born in the same year that you were. You have no choice but to spend your entire life with the members of your birth cohort. You and your fellow cohort members will share the same slice of history and be exposed to the same society-wide processes. You will not only be going through many of the same life transitions as they will be, but also you will probably be doing so at about the same times. Even though you will know only a few of them personally, the other members of your own birth cohort are important to you because you will be competing with them for much of whatever it is that you will ever want.

The process of thinking about your life choices from this perspective is valid regardless of your particular birth cohort. I have written this book so that everyone, regardless of age, can directly relate to the material presented. For the sake of clarity, however, I have focused on one cohort that has ahead of it all the life-course events discussed in the book—people born in 1968. I use the 1968 birth cohort to illustrate how birth cohorts, life events, and the sociological perspective can be applied to personal decision making.

If you were born a few years before or after 1968, the examples still apply but will differ only in your experiencing the various events that much sooner or later. If you were born several years, or even decades, before 1968, you can use the cohort approach two ways: (1) to gain insight into your own personal history; and (2) to make choices about those life events still ahead of you.

VIEWS ABOUT THE LIFE COURSE

Thinking about life as a series of events or stages is an idea at least as old as the ancient riddle of the Sphinx: what animals walk on four legs, then two legs, and then three legs before they die? The answer is human beings, who crawl as infants, walk as adults, and use a cane in old age. The riddle implies that life is a cycle with universal, biologically determined stages from birth to death.

Adult Development

Just as infants grow into children who, in turn, become adults, adults also continue to change both physically and mentally as they age. This perspective usually is called the adult development approach. It is concerned with life changes that are thought to: (1) accompany chronological aging; (2) be universal in all humans; and (3) be successive in that an earlier stage must always precede a later stage.

Because of its focus on biological and psychological processes of aging, the adult development view of life is held by many psychologists, physicians, and mental health workers. Some social psychologists and family sociologists, however, have broadened the perspective to include social factors. They point out that "adulthood," for example, is socially defined and is not merely a matter of physical maturity.

Adult developmentalists often prefer the term "life cycle," since to them the expression carries with it the idea of a set sequence of stages from birth to death. While not all persons taking this perspective believe that life changes are precisely tied to chronological age, a listing of life stages, such as the following, is characteristic of the approach:

Age	Developmental Periods and Transitions
0–3	Early Childhood
3–16	Childhood and Adolescence
17–40	Early Adulthood
40–60	Middle Adulthood
60+	Late Adulthood

The adult developmentalist believes that certain tasks must be accomplished at each stage in life. During the "early adult transition," for example, the primary tasks are to separate yourself from adolescent relationships and groups, and to consider and try out various adult identities. During your twenties, the exploratory period of keeping your options open encounters the contradictory task of deciding whether to make commitments to an occupational choice, to a spouse, and to your own children if you choose to have any.

By your early thirties adult developmentalists believe the trial period for many life choices is drawing to a close—that time is running out for beginning major life commitments. The structure of your life is taking shape. In your late thirties your task presumably is to fulfill the aspirations of your youth, and to develop the commitments you already have made toward your spouse, children, occupation, or community. Others expect you to perform, to undertake responsibilities, to settle down as a contributing member of your society. Adult developmentalists believe that serious personal problems are likely to occur if people have not successfully dealt with the tasks of entering the adult world, or of settling down.

The "mid-life transition" during your early forties involves the task of reevaluating the life structure you have created for yourself. Youthful aspirations may have faded. Commitments to your spouse and children may be changing. A serious illness, either your own or that of a close relative or friend, may change what you and others expect of your behavior. If you have created a viable and meaningful life structure by this time, adult developmentalists claim that the mid-life transition need not be a period of personal stress and crisis. It can be the foundation for a stable middle adulthood, and a secure late adulthood.

Life Events

The adult development approach is a useful means for gaining some understanding of what happens to you as you go through life. But what if you don't believe everyone must march through the same series of developmental stages, accomplishing the same developmental tasks? Fortunately there is an alternative view of the life course, one which assumes a greater range of personal choice—the life-events approach.

Unlike stages in life through which everyone presumably goes if they live long enough, many important events in life are a matter of choice. Since you can exercise some control over major events in your life and your transitions to and from various social roles, some argue that those matters should be the focus of your attention. Those events may be highly related with age for most people; the important point is that many are not inevitable.

The "life-events and role transitions" view (which, for the sake of brevity, I shall call the "life-events" approach) emphasizes social factors over biological or psychological matters. As such, the view is favored by many sociologists and demographers. It assumes that societies will differ widely regarding which events and role transitions are held to be important, and in their timing and sequence in the life course. The life-events perspective sees your own lifetime as a series of certain events, living arrangements, and activities, instead of the fixed set of predetermined stages proposed by adult developmentalists.

A marriage, for example, is not only an event, a ceremony, but also a transition from a social role as a single person to that of a married person. The birth of a first child changes its parents' social roles from being childless to being a mother and father. The death of both parents ends a person's role as a son or daughter. The life-events view emphasizes, but is not limited to, such matters as those listed in Table 1-1.

Table 1-1 Which Role Transitions Accompany Which Life Events?

Life Event	Role Transition FROM:	TO:
1. Completing your formal education	Student	Nonstudent
2. Your first full-time job	Nonworker	Worker
3. Your first marriage	Never-married	Married
4. Purchase of own home	Renter	Home owner
5. Birth of your first child	Childless	Parent
6. Birth of your last child	Childbearing	Post-childbearing
7. Divorce	Married	Divorced
8. Remarriage	Unmarried	Married
9. Marriage of your oldest child	Parent	Parent-in-law
10. Marriage of your youngest child	Childrearing	Post-childrearing
11. Birth of first grandchild	Parent/Parent-in-law	Grandparent
12. Death of one of your parents	Son or daughter	Part orphan
13. Your retirement from the labor force	Worker	Nonworker
14. Death of your other parent	Son or daughter	Orphan
15. Death of your spouse	Married	Widowed
16. Your own major disabling illness or accident	Independent living	Living in an institution

From the life-events view, you have a great deal of choice about what happens to you in your lifetime and when it does—you have many opportunities for being self-directing. You may decide never to marry or have children, or to change occupations, if necessary, to avoid retirement. Even if you do experience the same events in life that others do, you may be years, perhaps decades, early or late compared with the average. Or your events may occur in a different sequence than those of other people.

Role transitions can involve major shifts in the social institutions through which you live your life, drastically alter your personal situation, and possibly cause you to rethink long-held values and beliefs. A setback in your educational progress, for example, may alter your criteria for choosing an occupation. Or an unexpected pregnancy may force you to make family choices different from those you had been expecting.

The life-events view assumes that, as an adult, you can choose to prepare yourself for a forthcoming transition in your life. By anticipating your future role transitions, you can learn ahead of time what to expect and be ready for the transition when it does occur. This approach assumes that a continual learning of new adult social roles, called adult socialization, is part of living. Role transitions, even those involving losses such as retirement or widowhood, need not become personal crises. Problems can occur, however, when individuals find themselves in social roles for which they have not prepared.

Both major views of life as it progresses through the years—that based on adult development and that based on life events—have their advantages. Each emphasizes a different part of reality, and both have a contribution to make to your understanding of your future life course. This book will take ideas from both views. The adult development approach shows that physical, psychological, and social changes do occur as you age, and influence both your physical abilities, your psychological needs and desires, and your social options. The life-events perspective illustrates two seemingly contradictory facts of life: (1) within broad social classes, regions of the country, or racial or ethnic groups, most people do the same things at about the same age; and (2) you don't have to follow your group's norm for many important events in life. It also emphasizes that you need never stop learning new roles as you go through life.

COMBINING THE THREE PERSPECTIVES

Each of the three perspectives—sociological, demographic, and life course—can offer useful insights and information for making life choices. The practical value of the perspectives is greatly enhanced when they are combined to interpret government projections relevant to many events and transitions you will face (education, labor force, marital status, childbearing, housing, and retirement). Throughout this book I will show you how to locate your cohort in the projections. I also will help you better understand what a projection reveals about a certain life event or transition.

The following chapter will show you how population projections are made, and how to read and understand bar graphs of population projections. Once again, the population projections used in the book are not forecasts either of your future or that of your cohort. What they will show you, however, is the range of options open to you for a certain life event or transition, and the average ages in the nation at which they take place. The next step is to turn to sociological and life-course studies to discover the advantages and disadvantages of the various options. Knowing this, you will be better equipped to decide whether you want to experience that event or transition and, if so, whether you want to go through it earlier or later than average.

I have organized this book into chapters covering some of the more important life choices you will face. Your first set of major life choices involves the transition from adolescence to adulthood. For many people the expected order of events is first to finish their full-time formal education, become economically independent through full-time employment, and then marry and establish their own families. Not everyone, of course, does all these things or in that order. Increasing numbers of persons are blurring the transition by mixing a part-time student role with full-time work. Some marry before finishing their formal education or becoming financially independent. Some may never enter the labor force; others may never marry.

These events in life are discussed in Chapters Three, Four, and Five. Chapter Three, "How Much Formal Education?," examines the links between educational accomplishments, employment, and income. The two major life choices are: (1) how much formal education to complete; and (2) whether to devote most of your life to a career that requires higher education. The chapter includes a projection of lifetime earnings by educational attainment and gender for full-time workers born in 1961.

Chapter Four, "Which Occupation?," includes a projection by age and gender of the United States labor force in 1995. Young and middle-aged men have little choice in this matter—virtually all are expected to seek employment. Young women have a wider range of choices: full-time employment (regardless of marital status); combining a homemaker role with part-time employment; or being a full-time homemaker. In spite of their greater choice, by 1995 over four-fifths of women in their late twenties are expected to be in the labor force. Thus, occupational choices are important for both genders. Chapter Four takes up the matter of occupational values, and how the sexual stereotyping of some occupational fields is changing.

The third major life choice, "Married or Unmarried?," is considered in Chapter Five. The question is not only whether and when to marry for the first time, but also whether to remain married. I will show you the proportions of never-married, married, divorced, and widowed people that the Social Security Administration is projecting for your cohort in 1995. Using a sociological explanation of why most people marry, Chapter Five also explores social values about marriage and sexual ideologies.

Many important, adult, life-course events and transitions involve making decisions about with whom you want to live. Your living arrangements result from choices about marriage, having children, and your relations with your parents, brothers or sisters, or other relatives. You choose whether to live alone, with nonrelatives, or with relatives. One such choice, "Childfree or Parent?," is the focus of Chapter Six. It examines the most common age for having children, parenting values versus childfree values, and a projection of the kinds of households (family or nonfamily) projected for your cohort in 1995.

While people in their late teens and early twenties change addresses frequently as they make the first transitions to adulthood, most people in their early forties stay years in the same community because of long-term commitments to family life or to a job. Many middle-aged people have tried to create a certain way of life for themselves, and are midway in the process of living that life. Chapter Seven, "Homeowner or Renter? Mover or Stayer?," considers two aspects of the process. The chapter not only considers social values about renting versus home-owning, how population change may influence first-home buying prospects in the 1980s and 1990s, but also it explores who is most likely to change residences.

Americans today generally end their labor-force participation during their sixties. If you expect to do the same when you reach that age, you may want to reconsider your retirement assumptions.

About half of American men and three-quarters of American women are projected to live into their early eighties by the year 2040. If you live a life of average length, and yet retire in your sixties, you may face an important life choice during the last decades of your life—how to maintain your economic independence. Chapter Eight, "What Can You Expect in Retirement?," examines the question in relation to the aging of the large Baby Boom cohort (persons born from 1946 through 1964) being followed by much smaller cohorts, and the resulting large Social Security shortfalls being projected for 2010 and afterward.

The book's concluding chapter, "Making Choices in an Age of Uncertainty," summarizes the previous chapters while taking into account the fact that the future is largely unknown. As an example of the underlying life script being lived out by most of us, the chapter outlines when the 1968 birth cohort will be experiencing certain major life events and transitions. The chapter assumes that in spite of rapid social change, and in spite of the risk of societal collapse through nuclear war or environmental disaster, life, particularly your life, goes on. As you continue to live, you will reach certain age-related turning points—there is no avoiding them.

Potential societal disasters should not freeze you into inaction over your personal life choices, nor prompt you into acting impulsively. Regardless of what may happen to the world at large, by thinking rationally about your own life course, and by applying the sociological perspective to your decisions, you may commit fewer mistakes, be able to choose more intelligently, and feel that you have greater control over your life than you otherwise would.

2 /

Life Prospects and Cohort Size

Many people's more important life choices involve such questions as:

> What occupation should I pursue? And how should I prepare for it?
> Where will I eventually live? And will I be a homeowner there?
> What can I do to have a long, healthy life?
> What am I going to do about marriage and having children?

No one can avoid these questions—they are part of living. I believe answers to these questions are more easily found by realizing that millions of other people are facing similar choices. Their (and your) personal decisions about residence, death, and parenthood eventually produce the national rates of migration, mortality, and fertility. These three rates plus immigration into the nation will determine the total number of people with whom you will share your future, and with whom you will compete to realize many of your aspirations.

Your life prospects are influenced not only by the total number of people in the nation but also by the number in your particular birth cohort (all people born in the same period you were). You will be competing against your agemates for many things—education, jobs, housing, material resources, energy supplies, and clean air and water. You should have some idea of how much competition you will face and from whom—that is, how big your cohort is and how it compares in size with other cohorts. You also will want to know how big your cohort may be in the future.

The first step in knowing about your cohort is to become acquainted with demography (the study of human populations). The second step is having some basic understanding about how projections of future cohort size are made. The demographic approach links many of the biological differences between the sexes or physical changes brought about by aging to important social matters such as marriage, parenting, family composition, and widowhood. It presents these events numerically so they can be discussed precisely. Fortunately, demographic ideas are not difficult to grasp in spite of their numerical appearance. They are descriptive, straightforward, and concrete.

The first demographic skill I will show you in this chapter is how to read bar graphs showing the age and sex composition of populations (called "population pyramids"). Once you know how to interpret them, population pyramids can reveal to you the past, present, and possible future of a population. In following chapters, I will use population pyramids to picture your marriage options, your possible employment and family choices, and some of your retirement prospects.

The second demographic skill you will be introduced to is the ability to understand and use population projections. When talking about future possibilities, demographers are careful to state their assumptions. Only three processes—fertility, mortality, and migration—cause all population change. If so many people are born, so many die, so many move away, and so many move in, then the population will change by a certain number of people over a particular period of time. By making assumptions about how each factor will change, you can calculate the resulting increase or decrease in population size.

The facts about United States population trends I present in this chapter are available in standard government reference books listed in the chapter's references. In the interest of brevity and clarity, I have not cited specific sources and page numbers. But if you want to dig deeper into the sources (and I encourage you to do so), your best guidebook to United States government documents is the most recent *Statistical Abstract of the United States.* The detailed information you seek may be in the abstract's over 1500 tables. And if it is not, the abstract has an extensive appendix listing sources of statistics alphabetically arranged by subject matter.

UNDERSTANDING POPULATION PYRAMIDS

The population pyramid diagram is a powerful tool for understanding population processes. It connects persons of all ages and shows how the number of people differs by age and sex. The population pyramid of the United States in 1985, for example, is shown in Figure 2-1. You can find your place in this or any other population pyramid by figuring how old you would be at the date the pyramid represents. People born in 1968 would be seventeen in 1985, for example, and are included among those in the fifteen through nineteen age-group.

Population pyramids are simply constructed. Ages start at zero at the bottom of the chart and usually run in five-year age-groups up through "eighty-five and over" (an open-ended category at the top). Males are on the left side, females on the right, and the number (or percentage) of each sex runs along the bottom. A bar is drawn to show the number (or percentage) of people in each age and sex group. When all the bars have been completed for every age/sex group, the resulting drawing shows at a glance the age and sex composition of the population.

Major Causes of Different Cohort Sizes

The expression "birth cohort" may refer to everyone born in just one year (the 1968 cohort), or in several years (the Baby Boom cohort of 1946 through 1964). Some age-groups with unusually large or small numbers of people have been labeled in Figure 2-1 by their cohort names: the Roaring Twenties Babies, the Great Depression Babies, the Baby Boom Babies, and the Baby Bust Babies. If your birth year does not fall into one of these named cohorts, don't feel left out. It is simply the result of your having been born in a transitional year between large and small cohorts.

Higher death rates with advancing age cause a rapid decline in the number of persons in each age-group after age sixty-five. This is especially the case among men. The constrictions and bulges in the age composition of the rest of the population mainly result from wide swings in the number of children born in the past. The low fertility years of the Great Depression happened between two high fertility periods—the Roaring Twenties and the Baby Boom. The Baby Boom was followed in the 1970s by a decade of low fertility (the Baby Bust). Births are expected to increase during the 1980s as the Baby Boom Babies have their own children. I call the demographic echo of the Baby Boom the "Eighties Babies."

The changes in birth numbers are dramatic. During the fifteen years from the middle of the Great Depression to the early part of the Baby Boom (1935 to 1950), the number of births increased by fifty-three percent to 3.6 million. Fertility remained high all through the 1950s and early 1960s—in 1964 over four million babies were born. Then fertility began to drop suddenly. From the last part of the Baby Boom to a low point of the Baby Bust (from 1964 to 1973), the number of births declined by twenty-two percent. As the Baby Boom Babies began having their own children, the number of births increased once again—up sixteen percent between 1973 and 1981. The ups and downs in fertility in the United States were not unique. Many other nations experienced low fertility during the Great Depression, a period of high fertility after World War II, and low fertility during the 1970s.

Consequences of Different Cohort Sizes

The number of people born the year you were is a good example of a social process that has a great influence on your life but over which you have

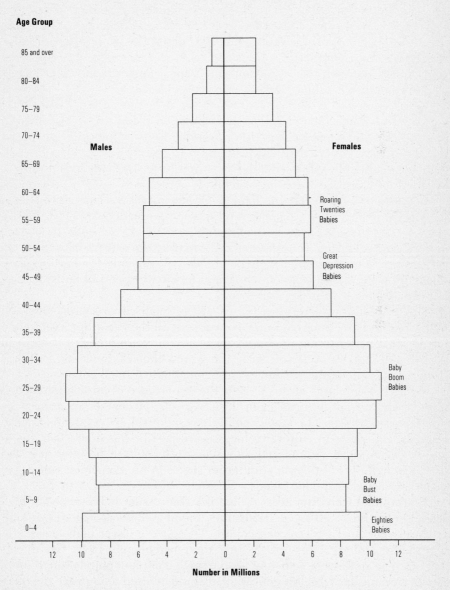

FIGURE 2-1 UNITED STATES POPULATION BY AGE AND SEX, 1985.

Source: U.S. Bureau of the Census, *Current Population Reports,* Series P-25, No. 922 (October 1982).

had no control. If you are a member of the Baby Boom cohort, the Depression cohort, or older cohorts, by now you have experienced many consequences of differing cohort sizes. If you were born after the Baby Boom, you have experienced some consequences—especially in education—but most are still in your future. Learning something about the experiences of older cohorts can help you better understand what you may expect. Comparing your cohort size with that of persons older and younger than you can show you how important cohort size is to life prospects.

Generally speaking, Baby Boom members are less fortunate in many matters than the much smaller cohort of Depression Babies. At every stage in life, they have had more competition from the larger numbers of people in their own birth cohort than did people ten to twenty years older. Beyond that, their suddenly greater numbers created huge demands for education, housing, and jobs that were not easily met.

If you were born during the Baby Boom, do not let the competition from the large number of your agemates make you feel inadequate. You did not choose when to be born. In spite of the importance of your cohort's size for most of your agemates, your particular life may be the exception to the average pattern. Knowing about general trends is invaluable for making decisions. But general trends don't determine the life prospects of individuals—individual choices do make a difference.

Similarly, if you were born in one of the small cohorts preceding and following the Baby Boom, do not give yourself all the credit for every good fortune that may happen to come your way. You were lucky to have been born at the right time. If you make the wrong choices, however, you may throw away some of the advantages of belonging to a small cohort.

While the emphasis of this book is the importance of population factors in your life, not all differences in life prospects, of course, are caused by different cohort sizes. Economic conditions, political events, technological changes, and shifts in cultural values all are part of the story. The demographic factors can be counted, however, so let us see how the ups and downs in numbers of people at different stages in life coincided with some major social and economic trends.

Educational Consequences   When the Depression Babies went to high school in the late 1940s and 1950s, they found an educational system built for the larger Roaring Twenties cohort. There were fewer high-school students in the United States in 1950 than there had been in 1940. Classrooms and teaching staffs were sufficient for the smaller student population. If more money became available for education, it could be used to improve the quality of schools instead of being used to provide more classrooms and teachers.

Twenty years later, in the 1960s and 1970s, the Baby Boom Babies reached high school. The number of high-school students more than doubled between 1950 and 1970. If you are an older member of the Baby Boom cohort, you may remember crowding into schools that had served well enough for the smaller number of Depression Babies. As Landon Y. Jones points out in his book about the Baby Boom, *Great Expectations*, the American educational system at first could not keep up. For many this meant attending school in double shifts, sitting in overcrowded classrooms, and learning from overburdened instructors.

The deteriorating classroom situation in elementary schools in the 1950s, and in high schools in the early 1960s, changed public perceptions about education in the United States. In the elementary grades in 1960, for example, there were twenty-eight pupils for every classroom teacher in public schools, and thirty-six pupils per teacher in private schools. The difficulty in meeting the demands of suddenly larger numbers of students contributed to a belief that a national educational crisis had developed.

During the 1960s and 1970s education received more support than ever before. True, important regional and central city/suburban differences in spending for education remained. Nevertheless, the proportion of the gross national product spent on public and private school expenditures from nursery school through higher education increased from 4.9 percent in 1960 to a high point of 7.6 percent in 1975.

The resources devoted to education went beyond those needed to merely cope with the increased numbers of students. By the late 1970s, far more money was being spent per pupil than during the late 1950s. The average yearly amount spent on each pupil in public schools doubled between 1960 and 1980, even holding inflation constant (from $1,250 to $2,500 calculating the cost in 1980 dollars). In public high schools over the same two decades, the average number of students for each teacher decreased from twenty-two to seventeen.

Was the educational crisis overcome? Yes and no. On the positive side, more students were staying in school at each level. Of all fifth graders in the United States in 1942 (a Depression cohort born in 1932), about half graduated from high school in 1950 and about one-fifth began college. But of all fifth graders in 1962 (a Baby Boom cohort born in 1952), three-quarters graduated from high school in 1970 and about half went on to college. Similarly high proportions graduated from high school and went on to college throughout the 1970s and early 1980s.

More blacks than ever before completed high school. Between 1950 and 1981 the proportion of high-school dropouts among young adult blacks declined from four-fifths to less than one-quarter. For young adults of all races the figure fell from half to one-seventh. In 1950 black education lagged far behind that of whites. Among people in their late twenties, for example, blacks had completed an average of 8.6 years of schooling in contrast with 12.0 years for whites. But by 1981 young adult blacks had almost caught up with whites in years of school completed—12.6 years compared with 12.8 years.

Another accomplishment during this period was an increase in the formal credentials of elementary and secondary school teachers. State teacher certification standards increased. Local school boards paid teachers with Master's degrees higher salaries than those with only Bachelor's degrees. By 1981 the upgrading of teachers' credentials was remarkable. As late as 1966, one-eighth of elementary teachers had two years of college or less. By 1981 this proportion had dropped to less than one in every 200 teachers. At the other extreme, the proportion of elementary teachers with a Master's or a six-year professional degree increased from one-sixth in 1966 to almost half in 1981.

A lack of college credentials was not a problem among high-school teachers—less than one percent had two years of college or less both in 1966 and in 1981. And even in 1966, about one-third of all the nation's secondary teachers had a Master's or six-year professional degree. But with greater financial rewards for more credentials, by 1981 over half of all high-school teachers had Master's or six-year professional degrees.

On the negative side, although more people were beginning college, they were not scoring as well on standardized tests. For whatever reasons, between 1967 and 1981 the scores of college-bound students declined by nine percent on the verbal test, and by five percent on the math test. The reasons for the declines in test scores are controversial and beyond the scope of this book. In any case, by the early 1980s educational concerns had shifted from meeting quantity demands to maintaining quality.

One reason for the change in attitude was a realization that the number of elementary-grade pupils had begun to decline—by eleven percent during the 1970s. It was only a matter of time before the smaller numbers of Baby Bust Babies worked their way through their high school and college years. Thus, the educational system that had been rapidly enlarged to serve the Baby Boom now became overbuilt and overstaffed for the smaller cohorts of persons born after the mid–1960s. The number of elementary classroom teachers continued to increase during the 1970s, for example, in spite of the reduction in the number of elementary grade pupils. As a result, the ratio of pupils per teacher in elementary schools improved from twenty-five to twenty-one.

The decrease in the number of students since the mid–1960s eventually caused the closing of some primary and secondary schools and the firing of many teachers. The proportion of the gross national product spent on education at all levels, both public and private, began declining from the 1975 high of 7.6 percent to 6.5 percent by 1981.

In money spent, student-teacher ratios, formal credentials of teachers, and the proportion of students going on to college, the educational opportunities for persons born in the 1960s and later have been and continue to be much better than those available to persons born in the early part of the Baby Boom years. If you were born in the late 1960s, you are (or recently were) making use of a costly educational system built to cope with the large birth cohorts that preceded you. This is just one example of how the size of your cohort can influence your life.

Job and Income Consequences By their early twenties, most people have finished, or are finishing, their formal education. They have jobs or are seeking work, or they are living in a household that includes a wage earner. This fact of life accounts for the high proportions of men in their early twenties in the labor force—over four-fifths percent between 1960 and 1981. The other men are full-time students, persons with major disabilities, inmates of institutions, and so on. Women in their early twenties have been less likely than men to be in the labor force. The proportion did increase from half to almost three-quarters between 1960 and 1981, nevertheless, as more young women postponed marriage and more young wives continued working after marriage.

The connection between age and full-time employment links cohorts with jobs and incomes. Your employment and earnings prospects are influenced both by the general economic conditions prevailing when you are in the labor force, and by your cohort's size. The effect of cohort size on labor force prospects can be better understood by seeing what happened to specific cohorts as they reached their early twenties. Let us compare the employment experiences of two five-year cohorts: (1) people born toward the end of the Great Depression (1936 through 1940); and (2) people born in the middle of the Baby Boom (1956 through 1960). The former were twenty through twenty-four years old in 1960, and the latter reached that age in 1980.

Persons born in the late 1930s were scarce when they came into the labor force in the late 1950s. Between 1950 and 1960 the share of the total labor force made up of people in their early twenties declined. Two decades later, however, the Baby Boom greatly increased the youthfulness of the labor force. By 1980, people in their early twenties accounted for fifteen percent of all workers, up from eleven percent in 1960. Their larger numbers increased the competition for jobs open to them.

One consequence was greater unemployment. Younger workers generally have higher unemployment rates than older workers. But when the Baby Boom members entered the labor force in large numbers in the 1970s, they found entry-level jobs in shorter supply than they may have expected. In 1980 the unemployment rate among people in their early twenties was more than triple that of people forty-five through sixty-four. Back in 1960, however, the situation had been more favorable for the Depression Babies seeking work. At that time the unemployment rate for young adult workers was about double that of older workers. Thus, one result of the smaller 1930s cohorts was a more even distribution of unemployment among all age-groups in 1960 when young workers were scarce. And one effect of the large cohorts of the 1950s was a concentration of unemployment in 1980 among younger workers who were in abundant supply.

Another consequence was lower income. Younger workers in 1980 earned proportionately less than had their older brothers and sisters who went into the job market in 1970. Younger workers generally do not expect to earn as much as older, more experienced workers. But by 1980 they were getting an even smaller share of the wage pie.

Here are the facts that show that. In 1970 men in their early twenties earned two-thirds as much money as that earned by men in their late forties and early fifties. Since older women do not earn as much as older men, young women get a bigger slice of the female payroll—in 1970 they earned nine-tenths as much as older women. Ten years later the Baby Boom members had filled the employment pipeline for young workers. The Depression Babies, furthermore, were moving into the more highly paid middle-aged years of life. The combination of abundant numbers of young workers and scarce middle-aged workers squeezed the incomes of the younger workers. In 1980 men in their early twenties earned only half as much as men in their late forties and early fifties. Among women the proportion was down to just over three-quarters.

Compared with the large Baby Boom cohort, the small Depression cohorts found employment more easily and received comparatively higher wages for their efforts. Competing with each other for available work, the Baby Boom members received lower wages and yet remained more vulnerable to unemployment than workers ten to twenty years older. Other things being equal, the advancement and promotion prospects of the Baby Boom members will continue to be slower and less promising than were those of the much smaller 1930s cohort members.

Housing Consequences   Your housing prospects, as your employment opportunities, result from both general economic conditions and your cohort's size. Birth cohorts are closely linked with housing trends because people generally first come into the home-buying market in their late twenties. Since 1976, for example, the average age of a first-home buyer in the United States has been about twenty-eight.

If you are in your early or mid-twenties, you may want to own your own home eventually. Chances are, however, that you are now renting or still living with your parents. It usually takes several years to save for the initial downpayment that makes homeownership possible. Your eventual home-owning prospects will be discussed in Chapter Seven. At this point, however, our interest is in better understanding how cohort size has been linked to home-owning prospects up to now.

People born in the 1930s were coming into the housing market for the first time from the mid-1950s through the late 1960s. Because of their small numbers, they created little additional demand for housing. New houses were built mainly to improve housing quality, not simply to provide houses for more new home buyers. As older structures were replaced with newer ones, the number of housing units in the nation built before 1940 declined by one-fifth between 1960 and 1970. The housing available to the Depression Babies in the 1960s was somewhat newer than that available to the Roaring Twenties Babies ten years earlier.

The initial waves of the Baby Boom cohort came into the housing market to buy their first houses in the mid– and late 1970s. Their much greater numbers, compared with the smaller 1930s cohorts, suddenly increased the demand for housing. Older housing was repaired and kept in service to help house the Baby Boom. Despite existing housing being another ten years older by the 1970s, the number of housing units built before 1940 declined only slightly (by three percent) between 1970 and 1980.

One result was that the proportion of newer housing units (built during the previous twenty years) among all housing in the nation declined slightly between 1970 and 1980. The housing attainable by Baby Boom members in the 1970s was a little older than that enjoyed by the Depression Babies ten years earlier.

The sudden change in cohort numbers also affected home prices. Because they put little demographic pressure on housing, Depression Babies found home prices moderate. Between 1965 and 1970, the median sales price of new, privately owned, one-family houses increased by seventeen percent— less than the twenty-three percent increase in the general consumer price index for the same five years.

Rates of inflation had increased greatly by the time the first Baby Boom members were reaching the home buying stage in the late 1970s. Between 1975 and 1980 the general consumer price index increased by fifty-three percent. During the same period, however, the cost of new, privately owned, one-family houses increased even faster—by sixty-four percent. The demographic pressure of the Baby Boom cohort on the housing market contributed to the rise in home prices. The Baby Boom members competed against each other to buy their homes, and bid prices up higher than they would have been otherwise.

The effect of cohort size on home prices can be separated from that caused by inflation by comparing the younger, first-home buyers with older, repeat-home buyers. Inflation is held constant in this comparison because both first-home buyers and repeat buyers experienced the same general inflation rates during the late 1970s. First-time and repeat-home buyers generally look for different kinds of housing. With the equity built up in their first house, and with generally higher incomes, the average repeat buyer purchases a more expensive house than does a typical first-home buyer. In 1976, the first year the information is available, the median price of a home was $50,100 for a repeat buyer and $37,700 for a first-time buyer.

In 1976 the average first-home buyer had been born in 1948 (the third year of the Baby Boom), and the average repeat buyer had been born in 1940 (the last of the Depression Babies). Between 1976 and 1980 home prices rose by sixty-three percent for the more numerous first-home buyers, compared with fifty-one percent for the older and fewer repeat buyers. Once again, the Baby Boom members were competing against themselves more intensely than did the Depression Babies, in this case bidding up the prices they paid for their first homes.

Many Baby Boom couples watched ruefully as prices of homes increased faster each year than the amount they could put aside for their initial downpayment. The proportion of first-home buyers who used savings and investments as the only source of their downpayment declined from almost three-quarters to half between 1976 and 1980. Those who could not afford a downpayment turned to their families for help. People who had relatives help them make the downpayment on their first homes increased from one-fifth to one-third in the late 1970s.

Less fortunate Baby Boom members gradually realized they were being priced out of the housing market and would have to scale down their housing aspirations. Housing prices were rising faster than incomes. Between 1976 and 1981 the cost of homeownership rose more rapidly than the general increase in the cost of living. The cost of renting, however, and for whatever reasons, was rising more slowly than general inflation rates.

Thus, the Depression Babies had access to newer housing at comparatively lower prices than did the Baby Boom Babies coming into the market ten to twenty years later. By the early 1980s, after taking inflation into account, some Baby Boom members found themselves paying higher prices for older housing. Renting had become a much more affordable way to meet their housing needs than homeownership. Not that they had given up their aspirations for homeownership—they just could not afford it at the moment. To afford owning their homes, they needed higher incomes.

Many couples tried to reach their housing goals and make ends meet by having wives continue working after marriage. The proportion of married women in their early twenties who were working or seeking work outside the home increased from one-third in 1960, to half in 1970, and to almost two-thirds in 1980. In 1960 most young wives were full-time homemakers and not in the labor force. By 1980, in contrast, most young wives were in the labor force.

What consequences will cohort size have on your life prospects in the future? The same logic we have used to interpret the 1985 United States population can be used to interpret the importance of the age/sex composition of any population, even projections of populations yet to come. The first step, however, is to construct the population projection itself. How many people, and of what age and sex, are expected to be sharing your life in the future?

POPULATION PROJECTIONS

From now to the year 2000, we can expect continuing large increases in the number of people living in the United States. At the time of this writing, the Bureau of the Census is projecting a United States population of 268 million for the year 2000. That is about thirty million more people than the 1985 population. And it is just over double the 132 million people living in the United States in 1940 when the Great Depression babies were still children.

The United States population in 2000 will include everyone who lived in the nation in 1985, of course, other than those who died and those who left the nation. The Great Depression babies will be in their sixties in 2000. The Baby Boom babies will be in their late thirties, forties, and early fifties. The Baby Bust babies will be in their twenties. And the Eighties Babies will be in their teens.

The population pyramid for the year 2000 shows how long-lasting differences in cohort size are (Figure 2-2). There are several reasons for this. First, future fertility does not affect the sizes of cohorts that are already born.

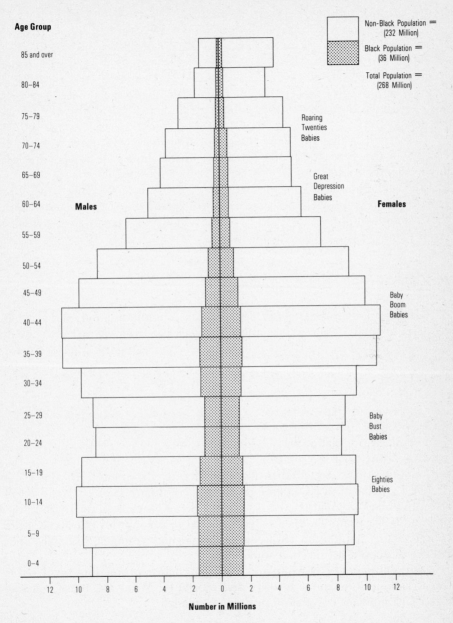

Age Group

85 and over
80–84
75–79
70–74
65–69
60–64
55–59
50–54
45–49
40–44
35–39
30–34
25–29
20–24
15–19
10–14
5–9
0–4

Non-Black Population = (232 Million)

Black Population = (36 Million)

Total Population = (268 Million)

Males

Females

Roaring Twenties Babies

Great Depression Babies

Baby Boom Babies

Baby Bust Babies

Eighties Babies

12 10 8 6 4 2 0 2 4 6 8 10 12

Number in Millions

FIGURE 2-2   UNITED STATES POPULATION BY AGE, SEX, AND RACE, 2000.

Source: U.S. Bureau of the Census, *Current Population Reports,* Series P-25, No. 922 (October 1982).

Future fertility adds people to the population only at one age—at birth. Second, mortality does not normally have much effect on the cohort sizes of children and young adults because few people die until they are middle-aged or older. And third, migration usually accounts for only a small part of the changes in the size of any given cohort. Unless altered by catastrophic changes in mortality such as war or plague, or huge movements of people across national borders, existing differences in age composition will persist for decades.

One result is that the Baby Boom cohort will remain the largest of all cohorts in the year 2000, and the Baby Bust cohort will be the smallest among people under fifty. The Eighties Babies show up clearly as children of the Baby Boom, an echo occurring about twenty-five years later. The cohorts in oversupply (1920s, late 1940s through early 1960s, 1980s), and those in undersupply (1930s and 1970s), probably will remain so throughout the lifetimes of the persons involved.

Projections of the Black Population

Besides population numbers, age, and sex, a population pyramid also has room for a fourth item of information. The only requirement is that the extra information must be available for each age and sex category. Figure 2-2, for example, shows the age and sex compositions in the year 2000 both of the total United States population and of a large minority group—black Americans. If you are black, you now can see how large your own particular age, sex, and racial group is. Thirty-six million blacks are projected for 2000, about seven million more than in 1985.

The black population has higher birth rates, higher death rates, and is growing faster than the white population. The proportion of blacks in the total population is expected to increase slightly between 1985 and 2000 (from 12.2 percent to 13.4 percent). Because of their higher birth and death rates, the black population also is younger than the white population. In the year 2000, for example, blacks are projected to account for one-sixth of the United States population eighteen years old and younger, but only one-twelfth of people seventy-five and older.

Differences between white and black population projections involve different assumptions about fertility and mortality. What are these assumptions? Just how are population projections made?

How Population Projections Are Made

Population projections systematically consider the future. They are not forecasts of what will happen, but merely "what if" calculations about what may happen. They are useful for setting reasonable limits to speculations about the future, and for showing us how the various "what if" assumptions interact with one another.

You can make population projections either by: (1) assuming current population trends will continue; or (2) assuming current trends in births, deaths, and migration will change. The former method is called the "straightline method" because it assumes trends over a certain period will continue in a straight line into the future. The latter approach is called the "component method" because it breaks population change into its three components—fertility, mortality, and migration—and makes assumptions about how each will change. Both methods have their uses. Both allow us to speculate systematically about the future. But neither method can forecast the future.

Straightline Projections   Using this method, you simply ask, "What if the population increases recorded between 1970 and 1980 continue unchanged through 2000?" Because the number of whites, blacks, and "persons of Spanish origin" (who may be of any race) were all recorded separately in the 1970 and 1980 censuses, a little simple arithmetic will produce projections of each group for the year 2000—if you assume the 1970 through 1980 trends will continue unchanged.

We can take the black population to illustrate this technique. Between 1970 and 1980, the number of blacks increased from 22.6 to 26.6 million—a 17.9 percent increase. If it continues growing at the same rate through the year 2000, there would be 31.4 million blacks in the United States in 1990 and 37.0 million in 2000. The arithmetic looks like this:

Year	*Number of Blacks*	*Increase at 17.9 Percent per decade*
1970	22.6 million	+ 4.0 million
1980	26.6 million	+ 4.8 million
1990	31.4 million	+ 5.6 million
2000	37.0 million	

The white population grew by nine percent between 1970 and 1980. If it continues to grow at that rate, there would be 233 million whites in the United States in the year 2000. Growing more rapidly than either blacks or whites during the 1970s was the Hispanic population—up sixty-one percent from 9.1 to 14.6 million. If this growth rate continues unchanged, there would be thirty-eight million persons of Hispanic origin in the United States in the year 2000.

At this point the usefulness of such simple calculations becomes apparent. If the black and Hispanic growth rates of the 1970s continue unchanged through 2000, the Hispanic group would replace blacks as the largest single minority group in the United States. And it would do so around the year 2000. (Some Hispanic blacks, of course, are found in both groups.) This is not a forecast that such a thing will happen. It is simply a systematic speculation about what may happen if the 1970 through 1980 trends continue.

Component Projections But I believe population trends are more likely to change than to continue in a straight line. I believe this to be true for whites, blacks, Hispanics, or anyone else. When speculating about future population trends, why not assume the trends themselves will change? By doing so, perhaps we can be more confident about any speculations we may make. And that is one advantage of the component method of making population projections—it allows us to make assumptions about how population trends may change. Another advantage of the component method is that it produces population projections of cohorts.

The population projections shown in Figure 2-2 were made using the component method. The arithmetic is much more complicated than that used for straightline projections and will not concern us here. What is important, however, is that you have some idea of the logic used in the component method. If you understand how such population projections are made, you are in a better position to judge for yourself how much confidence can be placed in the speculations you draw from them.

The component method involves starting with the number of people in each sex and age category in a population on a given date. You can start with a total population, or with a particular segment of the population such as a racial group. The projections shown in Figure 2-2 are based on starting populations of the estimated total number of people in the United States and the estimated United States black population on July 1, 1981.

The next step is to make assumptions about how you expect migration, fertility, and mortality to change. In fact, the most important things to know about component projections are the assumptions used in constructing them. You judge the usefulness of the projections by the reasonableness of their underlying assumptions.

I believe generally reasonable, middle-ground assumptions were used to project the United States population in 2000 as shown in Figure 2-2. The migration assumption adds just under half a million people each year to the population—a large number but one that does not include illegal immigration. The fertility assumption supposes an average of 1.9 births per woman in the future. This is a small family size but in line with recent fertility levels and with surveys asking young women how many births they are expecting. The mortality assumption is consistent with mortality projections made by the Social Security Administration.

Having made your assumptions, you then calculate how the resulting fertility, mortality, and migration rates will change the numbers of people in each age and sex group over the course of one year. Fertility will add a certain number of births that year to the bottom of the age/sex pyramid of the population. Mortality will subtract a certain number of people from each age/sex category that year. And migration will either add to, or subtract from, certain age/sex categories.

The combined result of all three factors produces the number of people in each age/sex category in the population at the end of that year. The 1981 population is projected one year forward to 1982. The process is repeated again to project the population for 1983. By repeating the process again and again, the projection can extend far into the future. The year 2000 projection used in Figure 2-2 is one of a series of projections made by the Bureau of the Census that includes other projections going on to the year 2050. The farther into the future the projection is made, of course, the more speculative it becomes.

I believe the population projection shown in Figure 2-2 gives us a useful base for beginning our speculations about life choices in the year 2000. We now have some idea of how many people to expect in the total population, in the black population, and in particular cohorts. The next step is to combine such population projections with projections about other areas in life. The following chapter takes up educational choices. The central issue is the level of educational accomplishment projected for cohorts and the sexes. Knowing this, you will be better able to decide how much formal education you may need to achieve what you want from life.

3 /

How Much Formal Education?

The lifetime personal value of a good college education cannot be measured. But some of the material benefits enjoyed by better-educated people can be documented—higher rates of full-time employment and higher incomes. The lifetime earnings of the better-educated are much larger than those of the less well-educated because the former generally are employed in full-time careers more consistently and have higher incomes. By "career" I mean an occupation that requires special training and in which a person hopes to make progressive achievements. A career offers more, and demands more, than a job done simply for an hourly wage or a weekly paycheck.

Although working full time is a necessity for most men and women, pursuing a full-time career is not. Even when they have the opportunity to begin (or to continue) a career, some people choose to work in a job just for pay, or to work part time. A two-earner married couple, for example, may earn enough income so that neither spouse need pursue a high-paying yet demanding career. Both spouses may be able to work in jobs that place only limited demands on them and that permit more time for family life, creative hobbies, travel, and other personal interests.

The matter of occupational choice will be taken up in the following chapter. This chapter's goal is to help you think about two related and continuing life choices: (1) whether to devote your working life to a full-time career that requires special training; and (2) how much formal education to complete. The growing numbers of older people who are returning to college, some because of changes in career goals, demonstrate the fact that educational choices made in a person's teens or early twenties are not necessarily final choices. For education, at least, the United States is the home of the second (and even third or fourth) chance to begin again.

Many believe, for example, that job and pay discrimination based on race, ethnicity, or gender can be overcome, at least in part, by achieving higher levels of formal education. The catch is that as more and more people become increasingly well-educated, more education is needed to keep ahead of the crowd. One consequence of this important social trend is that young adults without any college education are more disadvantaged today than ever before.

To assist you in thinking about your employment and educational choices, the following issues are addressed in this chapter:

1. How do expectations about full-time work affect educational goals?
2. How common is a college education?
3. Are male full-time workers better educated than female full-time workers?
4. Who gains more income by becoming better educated? Men or women? Blacks or whites? Which attribute is more closely linked with lower incomes—being black or being female?
5. What difference does age make? At what age is the income gain from higher education the largest? Does the gender gap in earnings narrow or widen with age?
6. What are projected lifetime earnings by educational level? How do they differ by gender?

EDUCATION AND VALUES

What is the value of an education? One of its greatest values certainly is in helping you become a more complete person—better able to think independently, define and achieve goals, and enjoy cultural treasures. In my opinion, the most important reason to continue your formal education, and to continue reading widely after you leave school, is to fulfill more completely your potential and interests.

Those fortunate enough to receive a good education, and those who read widely, increase their chances for enjoying richer personal lives. They can better express themselves in speaking and writing, analyze problems, interpret current events accurately, and appreciate the arts and sciences. In a word, a good education can help you better cope with the ups and downs of life—lifestyle choices, illness, pain, disappointment, political decisions, financial alternatives, and so forth. A broad education can invest your life with meaning and beauty that otherwise would be absent.

A college education that has great value for lifelong personal fulfillment, however, does not necessarily improve competitiveness for higher-paying careers. A four-year college degree is not an automatic ticket to a higher income. The occupation the degree leads to, and not the degree itself, produces the income. At the other extreme, an intensive, four-year vocational training program at the college level may yield a degree, good job prospects, and a higher income but little else in the way of enriching life. Some people are able to combine their occupational goals with a broad education while in college. Others experience a tension between their preferred college major and its marketability in the labor force.

How you choose to use your college education depends on the social values you have accepted. What will you do: learn more about yourself, your society, your cultural inheritance, your other personal interests; make the pursuit of a high-paying and marketable career the primary purpose of your college education; or find a middle ground between those two extremes? Social status in United States society is based, in large part, on education, occupation, and income. No wonder so many people feel strong social pressures to use their educational opportunities to enhance their chances for being employed in a high-paying career. But that is just one alternative among many.

Some highly vocational degree programs hope to broaden their students' range of knowledge by requiring them to take courses outside their major—including sociology courses. By taking sociology courses, or by reading books such as this one, a person may become a more effective school teacher, business manager, salesperson, health professional, or worker in virtually any other occupation dealing with people. Speaking as a sociologist, however, I believe the best reason to learn something about the sociological perspective is more personal—to have a better idea about what you are trying to accomplish with your life. Sociology can help you better understand the social reasons that, for example, you seek a college education in the first place, and why you may choose to pursue a full-time career.

FULL-TIME WORK EXPECTATIONS AND EDUCATIONAL GOALS

Persons less interested in full-time employment, regardless of gender and for whatever reasons, generally have less interest in furthering their formal educations. In past decades, work-related pressures to attain more education were felt more intensely by men than by women. Women could choose between marriage and full-time employment, and those planning to marry early had less reason to continue their education. For example, sociologist Margaret Mooney Marini surveyed over 6000 people in 1973–74 and found that a woman's age at first marriage was the most important factor limiting her education—more important than her high-school grades or her scores on standardized tests. Two other sociologists, Karl L. Alexander and Thomas W. Reilly, distinguished between schooling obtained before or after marriage. They also concluded that marrying early is detrimental to women's educational attainments but not to men's.

Many young women who did not expect to work full time for pay believed they had less reason to continue their formal education. In contrast, those who wanted full-time work in the labor force knew that their job opportunities would be better if they had more education. By 1981 the result was that among all women twenty-five years old and older, half of those with five or more years of college were employed full time and year-round compared with only one-third of those women whose formal education stopped with high-school graduation.

In recent years increasing numbers of women expect to be employed full time throughout their lives, and they plan to use their college years accordingly. Sociologists Mary C. Regan and Helen E. Roland found that since the early 1950s the most important life goals of women students at two major universities had shifted away from family relationships toward career or occupational pursuits. Even though such social pressures on women to work full time are greater today, women still have more choice in the matter than do men. Women have greater freedom than most men in deciding whether to work full time or to marry and depend (in whole or part) on their spouse's income.

If you are a woman the ideal time for making the choice about seeking lifetime paid employment is while you are still in school. You may wish to consider how your attitudes toward your education would differ (if at all) if you assumed that you would be in full-time, paid employment throughout your life. Ten or twenty years from now, for example, will you need to be self-supporting through divorce, widowhood, or never having married in the first place? Will you be solely responsible for supporting children or elderly parents? Or, even if married, will you want or need to be a major contributor to your family's income? Only time will tell.

If you are a man the social expectation to work full time is so strong that you may not even think about it as a choice. You may take it for granted that you must spend most of your adult life, say from your early twenties through your early or mid-sixties, in full-time, paid employment. But you also have choices in spite of social pressures to be self-supporting and, if married, to be your family's primary means of financial support. You can become a full-time homemaker if you marry and your wife agrees to pay the bills. Another option is to continue to work (perhaps less than full time), and to encourage and assist your wife to earn more than you do. If you did not expect to have to work full time, would you have a different attitude toward your education?

Whether man or woman, if you will be working full time the employment value of your education partly depends on how many other people are as well-educated as you are. How well-educated is your competition? Since you generally compete in the job market against others more or less your own age, it helps even more to know how well-educated workers are in your own birth cohort.

HOW COMMON IS A COLLEGE EDUCATION?

College education has become mass education in the United States today. In 1981 one-third of all whites twenty or twenty-one years old were still enrolled in school (part time or full time). And not quite one-quarter of all blacks the same age also were still students. Both figures are larger in 1981 than they were in 1960. At that time only one-fifth of whites and one-eighth of blacks in their early twenties were students.

College graduates are much less common among older people. Among people twenty-five and over, college graduates are more often found among males than females, and among whites than Hispanics or blacks. According to the United States Bureau of the Census, the proportions of white, Hispanic, and black adults twenty-five years old and over that were college graduates in 1981 were:

	Whites	*Hispanics*	*Blacks*
Males	22 %	10 %	8 %
Females	14 %	6 %	8 %

College graduates not only are more common among younger people, they also are more likely to be working full time. Should you need or want to look for full-time work, your competition is other full-time workers—not the general population. A relevant question is: how well-educated are full-time workers in your own age-group? It is still too early to know precisely how many of the people in their early twenties or younger eventually will become college graduates or full-time workers. The National Center for Education Statistics is projecting that from one-quarter to one-third of the 1968 birth cohort will be full-time or part-time college students when they are twenty years old in 1988.

If you are under twenty-five, a good way to get an idea of how well-educated full-time workers are is to examine the situation of people older than yourself. You can ask yourself if you want to be as well-educated as they are when you reach their ages. The most recent and reliable information about the educational attainment and ages of full-time workers in the United States comes from a March 1982 nationwide survey conducted by the Bureau of the Census. From that source, I calculated the percentages within selected age groups that had completed varying levels of college education (Table 3-1). I started with people in their late twenties and selected three more cohorts ten, twenty, and thirty years older.

Several important social trends and patterns reveal themselves in Table 3-1. Among older workers, men are better educated than women. The best-educated male workers had been born in the mid–1940s—one-third are college graduates and one-sixth have completed one or more years of graduate or professional school. However, while it is a highly educated cohort, it is also highly competitive. Men who never went to college find themselves much more disadvantaged educationally than are noncollege men born just twenty years earlier.

Educational levels among full-time workers generally decline more quickly with increasing age for women than for men. For example, most women workers born in the mid–1920s and who were in their mid– or late fifties in 1982 have not completed one year of college. Only one in eight is

Table 3-1   How Common Is a College Education Among Full-Time Workers?
Percentage Distribution by Educational Levels of Year-Round Full-Time Workers by
Gender in Selected Age Groups in the United States in 1982

| | Birth Cohort | | | |
	'53–'57	'43–'47	'33–'37	'23–'27
	Age in Years as of March 1982			
Gender and Years of School Completed	25–29*	35–39	45–49	55–59
MALE FULL-TIME WORKERS:				
5 Years College or More.	8%	17%	13%	11%
4 Years College.	17%	16%	13%	13%
1–3 Years College.	22%	20%	15%	13%
High-School Graduate or Less	53%	47%	59%	63%
Percentage Totals.	100%	100%	100%	100%
Total Men in Thousands . . .	(6,194)	(5,574)	(3,983)	(3,636)
FEMALE FULL-TIME WORKERS:				
5 Years College or More.	9%	11%	7%	6%
4 Years College.	19%	12%	8%	7%
1–3 Years College.	25%	20%	15%	15%
High-School Graduate or Less	47%	57%	70%	72%
Percentage Totals.	100%	100%	100%	100%
Total Women in Thousands	(3,844)	(2,779)	(2,192)	(1,820)

* = Many full-time workers at this age have not yet completed their formal education.

Source: Calculated from: Bureau of the Census, "Money Income of Households, Families, and
Persons in the United States: 1981," *Current Population Reports,* Series P-60, No. 137 (March
1983), Table 48, pp. 164, 165.

a college graduate. A female college graduate who was born in the mid–
1930s or before, therefore, enjoys a considerable educational advantage
over other women her own age.

Among younger full-time workers the situation is reversed—women are
better educated than men. The proportions of the Baby Boom cohort born
in the mid–1950s that are college graduates, or that have completed five or
more years of college, are somewhat larger among women than among men.
Over half of the women workers in this cohort have some college, and over
one-quarter have graduated from college. Almost one-tenth have completed
one or more years of graduate or professional school.

With so many full-time workers having had some college education, what
does it take to stay ahead of the crowd? The answer is clear if you were born
in the mid–1950s or later. To be in the upper quarter educationally of all
full-time workers in your age-group, you would need to be a college gradu-

ate. And if you wanted to be in the upper tenth, you would need to have a Master's degree or equivalent professional degree.

With so many—about half—of younger workers currently having had some college, does a college education still pay off in higher incomes? Yes, it does. But there are important differences by gender and race. Let us examine the facts in some detail.

WHO GAINS MORE INCOME FROM HIGHER EDUCATION?

Which Gender Gains More Income?

Given the differences between the genders in social expectations and personal values about seeking full-time paid work in the labor force, it makes sense to examine the links between education and income among people who are full-time, year-round workers. Regardless of gender, these workers presumably value or need full-time paid employment because, in fact, they are all working full-time. In the interest of brevity, throughout the rest of this chapter the word "workers" will refer to full-time workers unless otherwise noted.

The answer to the question, "Who gains more income from higher education?" depends on whether you are asking about dollar or percentage gains over people with less education. In 1981, men with higher education received greater dollar gains while better-educated women had greater percentage gains (Table 3-2). For example, comparing workers whose education stopped with a four-year college degree with those who did not go to college after graduating from high school, the total dollar gain for men was larger than that for women ($5,800 compared with $4,000). But the percentage gain for women was larger—thirty-three percent compared with twenty-eight percent for men.

Dollars and not percentages, of course, buy the groceries and pay the electricity bill. But the women's greater percentage gain is important, nevertheless, because women have lower earnings to begin with among high school graduates. What this means is that in order to have a higher income, education is more important for women than it is for men.

The contrasts were even more striking among workers with five or more years of college. Compared with workers with only a high-school education, the dollar gain was once again greater for men than for women. But the percentage gain in income was even higher for women than men—sixty-three percent compared with forty-eight percent.

Higher education did produce higher incomes for women, and slightly narrowed the gender gap in income. A wide income gap persisted, however—$10,300 among workers with five or more years of college. Among such well-educated workers women earned two-thirds as much as did men. Women with five or more years of college earned even less than did men

Table 3-2 Which Gender Gains More Income with Higher Education Among People Working Full Time?
Median Income in 1981 among Year-Round Full-Time Workers Twenty-Five Years Old and Over by Gender and Educational Level in the United States, 1982

Years of School Completed	Full-Time Male Workers	Full-Time Female Workers	The Gender Gap: Women's Income as a Percent of Men's
4 Years High School	$20,600	$12,300	60%
1–3 Years College	$22,600	$14,300	63%
4 Years College	$26,400	$16,300	62%
5+ Years College	$30,400	$20,100	66%
DOLLAR GAIN COMPARED WITH FOUR YEARS OF HIGH SCHOOL:			
1–3 Years College	$ 2,000	$ 2,000	
4 Years College	$ 5,800	$ 4,000	
5+ Years College	$ 9,800	$ 7,800	
PERCENTAGE GAIN COMPARED WITH FOUR YEARS OF HIGH SCHOOL:			
1–3 Years College	+ 10%	+ 16%	
4 Years College	+ 28%	+ 33%	
5+ Years College	+ 48%	+ 63%	

NOTE: Incomes are rounded to the nearest $100.

Source: Bureau of the Census, "Money Income of Households, Families, and Persons in the United States: 1981," *Current Population Reports*, Series P-60, No. 137 (March 1983), Table 47, pp. 156–163.

with high-school educations. Part of the gender gap in income among college graduates was due to different occupational choices many men and women make—a matter that will be discussed in the following chapter.

Which Race Gains More Income—Blacks or Whites?

The link between education and income involves the matter of the type of work done—whether a person simply has a job or has a career that pays increasingly greater returns as it develops. Using information from the late 1960s and early 1970s, sociologist Rachel A. Rosenfeld documented important race and sex differences in work patterns existing at that time. She found that the career profiles of women and nonwhite men were distinctly different from that of white men. Details about more recent white and black racial differences in education and income are available from the same 1982 Bureau of the Census survey that gave us information about gender differences. At the time of this writing, no such recent and detailed information is available for Hispanics, Native Americans, Asian Americans, or other smaller racial or ethnic groups.

Which attribute is more closely linked with earning lower incomes—being black or being female? The answer is being female. Whether white or black, women had lower average incomes than did men within each educational category (top half of Table 3-3). Among workers, white men had the highest incomes, black men ranked next, white women were third, and black women had the lowest incomes. Within each educational category, black men's incomes were about three-fourths as large as white men's. But women's average incomes (whether black or white) never were more than two-thirds as large as white men's.

Did higher education reduce the income gap between blacks and whites? The answer depends on gender. It would be "no" among male workers. On the whole, higher education did not greatly widen or narrow the racial income gap among male workers. Although dollar gains were greater for white male workers, black men and white men both received about the same

Table 3-3   Does Higher Education Reduce the Income Gap Between Blacks and Whites?
Median Income in 1981 among Year-Round Full-Time Workers Twenty-Five Years Old and Older by Race, Gender, and Educational Level in the United States in 1982

| | Male Workers | | Female Workers | |
Years of School Completed	Whites	Blacks	Whites	Blacks
4 Years High School	$21,000	$16,000	$12,500	$11,500
1–3 Years College	$23,100	$17,400	$14,600	$13,200
4 Years College	$26,900	$19,900	$16,500	$15,000
5+ Years College	$30,800	$24,000	$20,200	$19,400

THE RACIAL GAP: BLACKS' INCOME AS A PERCENT OF WHITES'

	Male Workers	Female Workers
4 Years High School	76%	92%
1–3 Years College	75%	90%
4 Years College	74%	91%
5+ Years College	78%	96%

NOTE: Incomes rounded to nearest $100.

Source: Bureau of the Census, "Money Income of Households, Families, and Persons in the United States: 1981," *Current Population Reports,* Series P-60, No. 137 (March 1983), Table 47, pp. 159, 163.

percentage gains in income with higher education. This means that education was as important for having a higher income for black men as it was for white men. Black men did improve their incomes with higher education, but no more than did white men.

Among female workers, the answer would be a qualified "yes." Comparing female workers with the same level of formal education, blacks earned almost as much as whites. Among female workers with five or more years of college, the median income of black women was almost equal to the whites' (ninety-six percent). Among such highly educated workers, black women had both greater dollar and percentage gains in income than did white women, compared with high-school graduates of the same race and gender. Some black women had used postgraduate college education to almost close the racial gap in earnings with white women.

WHAT DIFFERENCE DOES AGE MAKE?

Personal income generally increases with age up to a certain point and then levels off or declines. Part of the increase with age is due to the time it takes for careers to pay off in higher earnings. And part also is due to higher wages or salaries paid on the basis of experience or seniority. Generally speaking, the more education a person has, the longer it takes to reach the peak earnings stage of life and the higher those earnings are. Among male workers in 1982 who were high-school graduates, for example, average earnings peaked at $22,600 for men in their early forties. The earnings of male workers with five or more years of college, however, kept increasing through their working lives and peaked at $40,800 among men in their early sixties.

Earnings also increased with age for female workers, but the gains were much smaller than for men. Only among workers with five or more years of college did the older women earn significantly more than younger women. And even among these well-educated women, their earnings did not continue rising with age into their fifties and sixties as had those of men with similar levels of formal education. Instead, their earnings peaked in their late forties at $22,900 and gradually declined thereafter.

What accounts for the smaller payoff in earnings with age for women? Among the many possible reasons, four stand out according to sociologists Donald J. Treiman and Patricia A. Roos. First, to the degree that job and income discrimination against women occurs, the gains in earnings women otherwise would have received are reduced. A second possible reason is a difference between men and women in work experience or educational background.

A third possible reason is that women are much more likely than men to interrupt their full-time employment for family reasons. By so doing, women risk losing seniority on the job or making less rapid progress in a career. Continuity of lifetime work has been shown by Joyce A. Stevens and Roger

A. Herriot to be a determinant of earnings. Their research revealed that a break of five or more years in employment lowered annual earnings on reentry into the labor force in 1972 by one-fifth for women and by almost one-third for men (compared with earnings of similar workers with uninterrupted work histories).

Fourth, women earn less because they are concentrated in lower level, lower paying jobs. Fewer women than men are members of labor unions, for example, where earnings are linked with seniority. Women accounted for less than one-quarter of the twenty-two million dues-paying union members in the United States in 1978. Another example: school teachers generally earn less than business executives, but in the past far more women chose careers in education than in business. Half of the women earning a Master's degree back in 1968 took it in education. But only one-fourth of men's Master's degrees were in education. Less than one percent of women's Master's degrees were in business and management, but fourteen percent of men's Master's degrees were.

Things are changing, however. Today increasing numbers of young women are choosing to follow careers that promise potentially higher lifetime earnings. Of the 147,000 Master's degrees conferred on women in 1980, for example, eight percent were in business and management. That is more than eight times the 1968 rate. Partly because of such occupational changes among better-educated women, the gender gap in income is narrower among younger than older college-educated workers. As younger women move into higher-paying occupations, their earnings come closer to men's. Among college-graduate workers in their late twenties, for example, women earned three-fourths as much money as did men (Table 3-4). Compare this with the fact that well-educated women in their late fifties earned only half as much as men.

Social status in United States society is based, in large part, on occupation or income. This does not mean you must put status striving as the first priority in your own life. But if one of your major life goals is to earn more money as you grow older, then—whether you are male or female, black, white, or Hispanic—here are the life choices to make now:

1. Plan to complete five years or more of college.
2. Decide to work full time throughout your life.
3. Choose an occupation that rewards seniority and experience, or a career that offers potentially larger earnings as you progress in it.

LIFETIME EARNINGS PROJECTIONS

Up to now we have considered the links between education, employment, and income for particular years and specific cohorts. But what about a person's entire working life? Because full-time higher education delays full-time

Table 3-4 How Do Age and Education Influence the Gender Gap in Earnings?
Mean Earnings in 1981 among Year-Round Full-Time Workers by Gender and Educational Level in Selected Age Groups in the United States in 1982

	Full-Time, Year-Round Workers			
	25–29 Years Old*		*55–59 Years Old***	
Years of School Completed	MEN	WOMEN	MEN	WOMEN
4 Years High School	$17,200	$11,800	$22,700	$12,800
1–3 Years College	$18,200	$13,300	$25,900	$13,600
4 Years College	$20,100	$15,400	$34,900	$16,100
5+ Years College	$23,000	$18,000	$40,600	$21,000

	The Gender Gap: Women's Income as a Percent of Men's	
	25–29 Years Old	*55–59 Years Old*
4 Years High School	69%	56%
1–3 Years College	73%	53%
4 Years College	77%	46%
5+ Years College	78%	52%

*Workers born from 1953 through 1957.
**Workers born from 1923 through 1927.
NOTE: Earnings rounded to nearest $100.

Source: Bureau of the Census, "Money Income of Households, Families, and Persons in the United States: 1981," *Current Population Reports,* Series P-60, No. 137 (March 1983), Table 48, pp. 164, 165.

paid employment, years may pass before college graduates recover income lost while they were finishing their education. They accept this short-term reduction in earnings because they assume their long-term earnings will more than make up for it. Just how large is the long-term payoff from higher education? And what about the gender gap in earnings? Does it widen or narrow over a person's entire working life?

The total amount of money a person may earn before retirement—one's lifetime earnings—can be estimated by making certain assumptions. Such an estimate is not a forecast of what people will earn. It is a projection of what they would earn if certain assumptions persisted unchanged throughout the years involved. As conditions change, then the estimated lifetime earnings also will change.

About once a decade the Bureau of the Census issues estimates of lifetime earnings. The most recent was published in 1983 and was based on earnings data for 1978, 1979, and 1980. The underlying assumption was that the links between earnings and age, gender, education, and employment rates prevailing around 1979 would remain unchanged. Lifetime earnings estimates were not made for whites or blacks separately, or for Hispanics or other minorities. The estimates were given in 1981 dollars and thus do not take into account inflation's influence on future incomes.

If you are a man born in 1961 or later, and work full time, chances are good that you will earn over one million dollars if you go to work full time straight out of high school (Table 3-5). How much more income could you expect with five or more years of college? The answer is almost one-half million dollars more. Despite the greater number of college graduates, a college education continues to be a profitable investment of time, money, and effort.

The lifetime dollar return of higher education for women is less but still significant. If you are a woman and attain five or more years of college and then work full time, your lifetime earnings should be $955,000, which is $321,000 more than the earnings of a woman worker whose education did not go beyond high school. Higher education may not return as many dollars

Table 3-5   Which Gender Gains More Lifetime Earnings from Higher Education?
Projected Lifetime Earnings (in 1981 Dollars) through Age Sixty-Four by Gender and Educational Attainment of Full-Time, Year-Round Workers Born in 1961

Years of School Completed	Male Workers	Female Workers	The Gender Gap in Lifetime Earnings
4 Years High School	$1,041,000	$634,000	$407,000
1–3 Years College	$1,155,000	$716,000	$439,000
4 Years College	$1,392,000	$846,000	$546,000
5+ Years College	$1,503,000	$955,000	$548,000
DOLLAR GAIN COMPARED WITH FOUR YEARS OF HIGH SCHOOL:			
1–3 Years College	$114,000	$ 82,000	
4 Years College	$351,000	$212,000	
5+ Years College	$462,000	$321,000	
PERCENTAGE GAIN COMPARED WITH FOUR YEARS OF HIGH SCHOOL:			
1–3 Years College	+ 11%	+ 13%	
4 Years College	+ 34%	+ 33%	
5+ Years College	+ 44%	+ 51%	

NOTE: Lifetime earnings rounded to nearest $1,000.

Source: Bureau of the Census, "Lifetime Earnings Estimates for Men and Women in the United States: 1979," *Current Population Reports,* Series P-60, No. 139 (February 1983), p. 3.

to women as it does to men over a lifetime, but it still is an excellent investment.

Higher education does not narrow the gender gap in lifetime earnings. On the contrary, the gap widens from $407,000 for high-school graduates to $546,000 for four-year college graduates. It is not that women college graduates earn less than women high-school graduates—they earn more. The gender gap widens because, until now, the well-educated men earned so much more than did well-educated women. The gender gap in lifetime earnings can have serious consequences for women in retirement, as we shall see in Chapter Eight.

The lifetime earnings estimates are based on assumptions arising from the way things were around 1979. The more rapidly young women enter life-long, full-time work in higher paying careers, and as discriminatory practices against women in the labor force diminish, the more likely it is that the gender gap in lifetime earnings will narrow in the future. Should you choose to work full time, the next choice is selecting an occupation. And that question is the focus of the following chapter.

4 /

Which Occupation?

Your choice of an occupation ideally should result from your own combination of interests, talents, and goals. But will job openings in your chosen field be there when you want them? By learning something about the conditions that will affect those job openings, you can make better decisions now that will prepare you for the future. You can be more confident that you are making the correct choices. Your insights into the future job market also will help you understand the occupational choices of people close to you—including those of your spouse if you marry.

The outside forces affecting your occupational future are both social and demographic. Sociology helps us to realize that social pressures for status from parents or peers, or the sexual stereotyping of certain occupations, may lead us into jobs that actually are not suited to our own interests and abilities. Demography helps us understand how changes in the numbers of people in certain age-groups influence the demand for workers in entire industries. In addition, we must realize that full-time employment is only one stage in life—one with entry and exit points closely linked to age.

Although the purpose of this chapter is to help you think about occupational choices, your unique occupational choice is, of course, beyond its scope—there are literally thousands of occupations from which to choose. The topics selected for this chapter, nevertheless, may not only help you anticipate future occupational trends but also may increase your understanding of how social values and institutions influence work choices. The questions answered in this chapter are:

1. Which occupations for college graduates are growing most rapidly? Which are growing slowly, if at all?
2. How does population change affect job prospects?

3. Do men and women value occupations differently? Which college majors are most popular among men? Among women? Are sexual stereotypes about occupations changing?
4. Which women are most likely to be in the labor force—never-married, married, divorced, or widowed? How numerous are employed wives? How do couples gain when wives work outside the home?
5. Who will be working in 1995? Will more women be working in the future? How does employment differ by age and sex over the life course?

RAPIDLY GROWING, LARGE OCCUPATIONS FOR COLLEGE GRADUATES

For many people an attractive occupation is one with expanding opportunities. Growing occupations generally have more job openings and offer more rapid career advancement. But growth is not the whole story. The number of people working in an occupation also is important. A slowly growing occupation in which hundreds of thousands are employed can have more job openings because of turnover (resignations, firings, deaths, or retirements) than a rapidly growing but small occupation in which only a few thousand people are working.

Which large occupations currently are growing most rapidly? To answer this question, a labor economist, Patrick D. Walsh, compared 177 occupations employing at least 25,000 workers each. Walsh ranked each occupation for growth during the 1980s. He also ranked them for size, earnings, and employment rates. Then, based on an occupation's rank in each of the four categories, he gave each occupation scores of one through ten. For example, if an occupation was in the highest tenth of all 177 occupations in growth, Walsh gave it a score of "ten" for that category. If an occupation was in the lowest tenth in, say, earnings, it scored a "one." An average ranking produced a score of "five."

From Walsh's list, I took the twenty-two most rapidly growing occupations that generally require at least a four-year college education (Table 4-1). Those scoring an eight, nine, or ten for growth were selected and, within each of those scores, ranked according to size (from largest to smallest).

Which is the highest ranking occupation for both growth and size? No, it is not computer programming (which ranked third). It is professional nursing. Nursing also scores high (a nine), on having a low unemployment rate. And even though earnings of nurses are not high, they are above average. As might be expected, besides computer programming another computer-related field ranked among the top three occupations—systems analysis. Both that field and computer programming pay well, have low unemployment rates, and today are large occupations employing many thousands of people.

Table 4-1 Twenty-Two Large and Growing Occupations for College Graduates

| | Ranking among 177 Large Occupations* | | | |
| | | | | EMPLOYMENT |
Occupation	GROWTH	SIZE	EARNINGS	RATE
Most Rapidly Growing Occupations:				
1. Professional Nurse	10	10	6	9
2. Systems Analyst	10	7	10	10
3. Computer Programmer	10	7	9	9
4. Aero-Astronautic Engineer	10	4	10	10
5. Physical Therapist	10	2	5	7
6. Speech and Hearing Clinician . .	10	2	5	7
7. Economist.	10	1	10	8
8. Recreation Therapist	10	1	5	7
Next Most Rapidly Growing Occupations:				
9. Electrical Engineer	9	8	10	10
10. Medical Laboratory Technologist	9	5	5	7
11. Architect.	9	4	9	8
12. Veterinarian	9	2	9	10
13. Dietitian	9	2	5	6
Other Occupations Growing Much Faster Than Average:				
14. Physician	8	9	10	10
15. Lawyer	8	9	10	10
16. Accountant.	8	9	8	8
17. Mechanical Engineer	8	7	10	9
18. Civil Engineer	8	7	10	9
19. Industrial Engineer	8	6	10	9
20. Securities Sales Agent	8	4	10	9
21. Psychologist	8	4	9	9
22. Geologist	8	2	10	10

*All occupations employed at least 25,000 workers in 1980. Ranks reflect deciles—"10" means top 10 percent among 177 occupations. A score of "9" means next 10 percent, and so forth. A score of "5" is average, while a score of "1" means lowest 10 percent.
GROWTH = Projected employment change between 1980 and 1990 (10 = most rapidly growing occupations).
SIZE = Number of people employed in the occupation in 1980 (10 = largest occupations).
EARNINGS = Average weekly earnings from 1979 through 1981 (10 = highest earnings).
EMPLOYMENT RATE = Average from 1972 through 1981 (10 = lowest unemployment rates).

Source: Patrick D. Walsh, "Comparing Occupations: Four Measures," *Occupational Outlook Quarterly* (Fall 1982), Vol. 26, No. 3, pp. 27–30.

Any of the top ranking twenty-two occupations should be considered as very attractive for growth and size. In addition, and partly because of the growing demand for them, all the occupations listed provide much better than average security against unemployment (except dietitian, whose unemployment rate still is above average). If you want to work in a large, growing field with low unemployment, and your desired or current occupation is listed in Table 4-1, you should consider yourself fortunate. Because of the attractiveness of these occupations, however, you can expect stiff competition in obtaining the training required to gain entry to them, and later in establishing yourself on the job. Because the careers are so competitive, not all law or medical students, for example, become successful and prosperous lawyers or physicians.

Growing demand does not necessarily produce high earnings. But, in fact, sixteen of the occupations listed also provide high earnings (scoring an eight, nine, or ten), mainly because they are all professional or technical fields. None of the occupations listed provides below average earnings (a score of four or less).

SLOWLY GROWING OCCUPATIONS FOR COLLEGE GRADUATES

Just as there are occupations growing faster than average, some occupations are growing only slowly—if at all. Which occupations are these? The most slowly growing occupations for college graduates are presented in Table 4-2. These eleven occupations scored a three or less in growth on Walsh's list of 177 large occupations. Within each growth category, I ranked the occupations in reverse order based on size (from smallest to largest). If your occupational choice is one of those listed, you should be aware that job openings during the 1980s will come more from turnover than from growth.

In growth and size, the least promising occupation is forester and conservationist: it scored a one on both criteria. Some jobs will open for foresters and conservationists during the 1980s because of turnover, of course, but opportunities generally will be limited. The three other lowest ranking occupations all involve teaching or library work—librarian, college or university teacher, and secondary school teacher. If you are interested in one of these large occupations, then at least you can take comfort from knowing that their size alone will produce some job openings for newcomers to meet replacement needs.

The eleven slowly growing occupations show how weak the connection is between earnings and an occupation's size or growth rate. In spite of their comparatively poor prospects for job openings during the 1980s, all eleven occupations pay well. In fact, seven even provide high earnings (scores of nine or ten)—pharmacists and airplane pilots are the best examples. Low growth in a high-paying occupation often means high levels of competition among newcomers for the few jobs that do open.

Your particular occupational interest may not be listed either among the twenty-two most rapidly growing jobs, or among the eleven most slowly growing. If so, you may be curious about how it stands in growth and size. You may find the answer in the most recent edition of a reference called by

Table 4-2   Eleven Large but Slowly Growing (or Declining) Occupations for College Graduates

| | Ranking among 177 Large Occupations** | | | |
Occupation	GROWTH	SIZE	EARNINGS	EMPLOYMENT RATE
Most Slowly Growing (or Declining) Occupations:				
1. Forester and Conservationist.......	1	1	6	3
2. Librarian........................	1	6	6	8
3. College and University Teacher	1	9	9	8
4. Secondary School Teacher	1	10	7	9
Next Most Slowly Growing Occupations:				
5. Biological Scientist...............	2	3	9	9
6. Pharmacist	2	6	10	10
7. Designer	2	7	9	7
Other Occupations Growing Much More Slowly Than Average:				
8. Airplane Pilot....................	3	4	10	8
9. Adult Education Teacher..........	3	5	8	5
10. Personnel and Labor Relations Specialist	3	7	9	7
11. Purchasing Agent and Buyer	3	7	9	8

**See Table 4-1 for definitions of rankings.

Source: Patrick D. Walsh, "Comparing Occupations: Four Measures," *Occupational Outlook Quarterly* (Fall 1982), Vol. 26, No. 3, pp. 27–30.

some the "book of jobs"—*The Occupational Outlook Handbook.* Hundreds of specific occupations are described in detail, including information about growth, size, earnings, unemployment rates, and required educational background. The book is published by the United States Bureau of Labor Statistics and written as a guide for the general public. It is available at most public libraries and many colleges.

HOW POPULATION CHANGE AFFECTS JOB PROSPECTS

Why do some occupations grow more rapidly than others? Employment opportunities change with three major forces: (1) ups and downs in the economy; (2) technological innovations that create new jobs while rendering other occupations obsolete; and (3) changes in the total size, age composition, and geographic distribution of a nation's population.

The first two forces receive considerable attention by the mass media. High interest rates for loans, for example, reduce the demand for things people usually borrow money to buy, such as cars and houses. As a consequence, high interest rates can reduce the demand for automobile assembly workers and carpenters. Computers are a recent example of how technological change can influence employment. The computerization of a bank, for instance, simultaneously reduces the need for bookkeepers while increasing the need for data-entry clerks.

The third force—population change—rarely makes the news. Under certain circumstances, however, it can be as important as economic and technological changes in determining why some occupations grow more rapidly than others. For our present purposes, let us focus on the ways in which population changes may affect job prospects during the 1980s and beyond.

If you look closely at the list of twenty-two rapidly growing occupations for college graduates (Table 4-1), you will notice that health fields and engineering are both overrepresented. Besides nursing, there are five other human health fields—physical therapist, speech and hearing clinician, medical laboratory technologist, dietitian, and physician. There are five rapidly growing engineering fields—aero-astronautic, electrical, mechanical, civil, and industrial. Technological change may account for the growing demand for engineers. But why the increased need for health workers?

Age Structure and Job Openings

The health care needs of a growing and aging population lead to an increased demand for nurses and other medical professionals. During the 1980s the United States total population is projected to grow by ten percent, and the older population (people sixty-five and over), by twenty-five percent. Add to that demographic demand the need for highly trained workers caused by advances in medical technology, and it is easy to see why medical care is considered a growth area.

The number of nurses, for example, is expected to grow by at least forty percent during the 1980s to over 1.5 million by 1990. The Department of Labor projects that increased demand alone will produce at least 44,000 new job openings for nurses each year during the 1980s. Even more job openings will be created to replace nurses who will leave the labor force for family or other reasons. In fact, three of four nursing job openings will be created by turnover. All told, an average of at least 180,000 jobs in nursing should open each year during the 1980s.

While job opportunities should be plentiful in nursing and other health fields because of a combination of demographic and technological forces, the opposite will be true of most teaching occupations. As we have seen, four of the eleven most slowly growing large occupations for college graduates involve teaching or library work (Table 4-2).

Population change is the most important reason for the bleak prospects for teaching during the 1980s. The numbers involved are large and the changes dramatic. By 1990 there will be seven million fewer people of high school and college age in the nation than there were in 1980—a decline of sixteen percent. In some northeastern and midwestern states, the drop will be even greater (perhaps as large as a one-third decline) because of regional differences in past fertility and current migration patterns.

The smaller number of people of high school and college age in the 1980s is a delayed consequence of the drop in the number of births between the early 1960s and the early 1970s. As the high school and college age population declines during the 1980s, the demand for teachers of teenagers and young adults will diminish. There will be between eleven and fourteen percent fewer high-school, college, and university teachers in 1990 than there were in 1980.

The rise in the number of births after the mid–1970s means that teachers of kindergarten and elementary pupils will be in a somewhat more favorable situation by the late 1980s. The National Center for Education Statistics projects that elementary school enrollments will begin to rise again after the early 1980s. In spite of the slightly greater demand for elementary teachers expected by the late 1980s, replacement needs still will produce almost nine out of every ten openings in the field between 1980 and 1990.

Health fields and teaching illustrate the importance of population change for job prospects in certain occupations. You may want to ask yourself if your own preferred occupation serves people of a certain age, or people at a particular stage in life. If so, chances are that job prospects in that occupation are influenced by changes in the total number of people it serves. By referring to population projections that give details about age and sex (such as those presented in this book), you can see for yourself whether the age-group your occupation serves is growing or declining in size, and when the changes are expected to take place. With this knowledge, you can better make your own career plans.

Your Own Cohort's Size

When thinking about your own occupational choices, you may want to consider not only how population changes affect certain occupations but also where your own birth cohort fits in. How large is your cohort? Where is it compared with the Baby Boom? (You can find the answers to these two questions in the illustration of the age and sex distribution of the United States in 1985—Figure 2-1 in Chapter 2).

If you were born in the late 1960s, for example, you will face less competition for your first job than did members of the Baby Boom because your cohort is smaller than that of people ten years older than you. But because you are being followed by even smaller cohorts, your job prospects in fields serving people ten years younger than yourself (such as secondary education) may be no better than were those of the Baby Boom members. They could be even worse if Baby Boom members take up the available jobs and hold on to them until they retire. In this way the Baby Boom members fill up career pipelines and slow the progress of people younger than themselves.

If you were born after the Baby Boom you may want to consider those occupations—such as health fields—that serve people ten or twenty years older than yourself. Other things being equal, you would be better off taking advantage of the large numbers of people born during the Baby Boom instead of competing with them. In this way, you could become a beneficiary instead of a victim of the Baby Boom.

The Number of College Graduates

Another important population factor affecting your own job prospects is the number of people who are better educated than you. The previous chapter described the remarkable increase in the number of college-educated people among younger full-time workers. The number of bachelor's degrees awarded annually, for example, increased from one-half million during the mid–1960s to almost one million by 1980.

No one can be over educated in terms of fulfilling personal potential or being a contributing citizen in a community. But it is possible to graduate more foresters, librarians, or teachers, as cases in point, than there are entry-level jobs in their chosen fields. This happened in many fields in the 1970s and probably will continue to happen during the 1980s and early 1990s.

So many college graduates came into the labor force during the 1970s that entry-level job openings for them did not keep pace. During that decade the college-graduate labor force grew by eighty-five percent—much faster than the growth of the total labor force (which grew by one-third). As a result, fewer college graduates were employed in professional and technical jobs. More found work in occupations that did not require a college degree—retail sales, service, farm, and blue-collar jobs. The federal Department of Labor estimates that one-fifth of all college graduates who entered the labor force during the 1970s either took a job that did not require a college degree or experienced unemployment.

Labor economist Jon Sargent expects that job prospects for college graduates entering the labor force during the 1980s will be similar to those of the 1970s—which means a surplus of college graduates. During the 1980s slightly more bachelor's degrees are expected to be awarded annually than was the case during the 1970s. Part of the increase will be due to younger Baby Boom members completing their degrees, and part will result from older workers returning to college. During the 1980s, nine million new college graduates are expected to enter the labor force seeking work. In addition, six million college graduates who previously had left the labor force (for family reasons or for advanced education) will be reentering.

If fifteen million college graduates will be added to the labor force between 1980 and 1990, how many job openings requiring a college graduate will be there for them?; not enough. Depending on the assumptions made about the economy generally and the growth in college-graduate-dominated occupations, from twelve to thirteen million entry-level job openings for college graduates are expected during the 1980s. Seven million openings will come from replacement needs, and the remaining five to six million from the growth of the economy or of particular occupations. Thus, there will be a surplus of two or three million more college graduates looking for jobs than the available number of entry-level jobs needing persons with a college degree.

The result will be that some college graduates, perhaps as many as one in five, may not find jobs in their chosen occupations. They can expect periods of unemployment, job-hopping, and relocating to other parts of the country before finding a satisfactory job. In spite of the competition among college graduates for preferred jobs, as a group college graduates will continue to have an advantage over workers without a college degree. Even if a job does not require a college education, many employers prefer to hire better-educated workers.

College graduates who make wise career choices, and who prepare themselves to enter the labor force while still in college, should have the best chances for finding employment in their chosen fields. As suggested earlier, a wise occupational choice takes into account the number of people working in the field and its projected growth. But even more important than these demographic factors is the match between what you want from a job and what the job requires of you—between your occupational values and a job's requirements.

OCCUPATIONAL VALUES AND JOB REQUIREMENTS

What do you want from working? Do you want to earn a high income? Or would you be satisfied with more modest earnings if you could spend more time on other interests—including hobbies, sports, family activities, civic or church activities? Another job consideration involves whether you want to have someone tell you what to do. How much close supervision of your own work do you want? Would you rather be the supervisor or the supervised? Your responses to these questions reflect some of your occupational values—the criteria you use for choosing an occupation.

To help you think about your occupational values, I have listed in a brief questionnaire format these and a few other things that some people want from their jobs (Questionnaire A). The criteria included, of course, are only a fraction of all the possible values people have about working. What you want from a job may not be on the list. Or you may desire a job allowing you to do all eight things listed. There is no correct set of responses. Each of us is different.

The questionnaire's purpose is to highlight the importance of values when making occupational choices. It is no substitute for the detailed personal surveys available through occupational counselors. Completing the questionnaire, nevertheless, may improve your understanding of just what it

QUESTIONNAIRE A: **Personal Questionnaire About Selected Occupational Values**

	I Strongly Reject				I Strongly Desire
	1	2	3	4	5
I WANT A JOB THAT ALLOWS ME TO:					
1. Earn a high income	___	___	___	___	___
2. Work without close supervision	___	___	___	___	___
3. Solve problems, be creative	___	___	___	___	___
4. Work part time if I choose	___	___	___	___	___
5. Organize, supervise, or persuade others	___	___	___	___	___
6. Help or instruct others	___	___	___	___	___
7. Have frequent public contacts	___	___	___	___	___
8. Use mathematics beyond algebra	___	___	___	___	___

Source: Adapted from Gail M. Martin and Melvin C. Fountain, "Matching Yourself with the World of Work," *Occupational Outlook Quarterly* (Winter 1982), Vol. 26, No. 4, pp. 2–12.

is that you want from a job. In spite of the strong social pressures to work to support yourself, you retain a considerable amount of freedom to choose the kind of work you do.

Once you have an idea of some occupational values that are important to you, your next step is to match your values with the requirements of particular occupations. Jobs requiring a college degree generally interest people desiring the first three occupational values listed in Questionnaire A. College-graduate jobs commonly provide good incomes, assume an ability to work without close supervision, and involve problem solving and creative thinking. College-graduate jobs differ widely, however, in the last five values on that list—working part time, organizing others, helping others, contacting the public, and using higher mathematics.

I have taken those five values and matched them with the job requirements of seventeen college-graduate occupations (Table 4-3) selected from a list of 250 jobs studied by Gail M. Martin and Melvin C. Fountain, staff writer and editor, respectively, of the *Occupational Outlook Quarterly*. The jobs and the job requirements have been arranged to put similar occupations next to each other. The seventeen jobs were selected to represent a wide

Table 4-3   Requirements and Characteristics of Selected Occupations Generally Requiring a College Degree

Occupation	Job Requirement or Characteristic				
	A	B	C	D	E
1. Writers and Editors	✓✓✓	✓✓✓	—	—	—
2. College Faculty	✓✓✓	✓✓✓	✓✓✓	✓✓✓	—
3. Librarian	✓✓✓	✓✓✓	✓✓✓	✓✓✓	—
4. Elementary School Teacher	✓✓✓	✓✓✓	✓✓✓	✓✓✓	—
5. Registered Nurse	✓✓✓	✓✓✓	✓✓✓	✓✓✓	—
6. Dietitian	✓✓✓	✓✓✓	✓✓✓	✓✓✓	—
7. Lawyer	—	✓✓✓	✓✓✓	✓✓✓	—
8. Personnel Specialist	—	✓✓✓	✓✓✓	✓✓✓	—
9. Secondary School Teacher	—	✓✓✓	✓✓✓	✓✓✓	—
10. Manufacturer's Sales Representative	—	✓✓✓	✓✓✓	—	—
11. Accountant	—	—	✓✓✓	✓✓✓	—
12. Psychologist	—	—	✓✓✓	✓✓✓	—
13. Sociologist	—	—	—	✓✓✓	—
14. Architect	—	—	—	✓✓✓	—
15. Computer Systems Analyst	—	—	✓✓✓	—	✓✓✓
16. Civil Engineer	—	—	—	—	✓✓✓
17. Chemist	—	—	—	—	✓✓✓
YOUR RESPONSES FROM QUESTIONNAIRE "A"	...	...	...	...	...
(Item Number in Questionnaire A)	#4	#5	#6	#7	#8

A = Part-time work available.
B = Organize, supervise, or persuade others.
C = Help or instruct others.
D = Frequent public contacts.
E = Use mathematics beyond algebra & trigonometry.
✓✓✓ = Required by, or characteristic of, occupation.
— = Not generally required by, or characteristic of, occupation.

Source: Adapted from Gail M. Martin and Melvin C. Fountain, "Matching Yourself with the World of Work," *Occupational Outlook Quarterly* (Winter 1982), Vol. 26, No. 4, pp. 2–12; and Gail M. Martin, "Math and Your Career," *Occupational Outlook Quarterly* (Summer 1983), Vol. 27, No. 2, pp. 28–31.

range of interests, abilities, and working conditions. Given the brevity of the list, you may not find on it the particular occupation in which you are interested. If so, you may wish to consider the occupation listed that comes closest to your own general interests.

I have included a space in Table 4-3 for you to transfer your own occupational values from Questionnaire A. Do your preferences match those of any of the occupations listed? Is that occupation the one for which you are preparing yourself? If so, your occupational values and the requirements of your preferred career are consistent. The match of occupational values and job requirements is what counts. Chances are you will like the work involved. And liking the work increases the odds that you will do well in the occupation.

But what if your occupational values more closely fit the needs of a job different from the one for which you are preparing yourself? What if, for example, you would really like being a nurse, but you are studying to become an engineer? In that case, what you want from a job does not match the requirements of the occupation you are seeking. Is the gap large enough for you to consider switching to a field more in line with your own interests, abilities, and talents?

Before you answer, you may want to ask yourself whether your occupational choice, or your occupational values, are in any way the result of sexual stereotypes. Career educator Mary Ellen Verheyden-Hilliard reports that most elementary-age students do not believe that opportunities exist for them in fields traditionally dominated by members of the opposite sex. This false belief becomes a self-fulfilling prophecy when boys and girls, and later men and women, do not take the educational programs, both in high school and in college, that eventually lead to specific careers. Sociologists Paul Lindsay and William E. Knox have documented the way in which work values influence educational attainment which, in turn, affects occupational opportunities and choices.

OCCUPATIONAL VALUES AND GENDER

A bachelor's degree does not necessarily indicate a specific occupational choice, of course, because many careers require formal education beyond a four-year degree. The major chosen by an undergraduate college student, nevertheless, can reflect both a person's occupational values and talents, and also sexual stereotyping learned as a child and a young adult from one's parents and peers. Thus, a listing of popular college bachelor's degrees earned by women and men can show how individual choices and social pressures combine to connect gender with certain fields (Table 4-4). Eleven popular college majors accounted for over half of all bachelor's degrees granted to women in 1980. Men were even more concentrated in a completely different list of academic majors. One field alone, business and management, granted one-fifth of all men's bachelor's degrees.

Why the contrasting gender choices in college majors? According to sociologist A. Regula Herzog, women generally prefer fields that allow them to work with people (interpersonal relations), to help others (altruism), and to express themselves (self-actualization). Men are more likely to prefer jobs that offer high material rewards (earnings). Two sociologists, Jeylan T. Mortimer and Jon Lorence, argue that work values about creativity, expression of interests, and being people-oriented, lead to jobs offering "intrinsic

Table 4-4   Popular College Majors among Men and Women College Graduates in 1980
Bachelor's Degrees Conferred in the United States in 1980 by Field of Study and Gender

Field of Study	Popularity for Women (Number of Degrees Conferred on Women)	Gender Gap (Percent in Field Conferred on Men)
POPULAR MAJORS TAKEN MAINLY BY WOMEN:		
1. Education (except Elementary and Physical)	39,400	29%
2. Elementary Education	37,700	10%
3. Nursing	30,600	6%
4. Psychology	26,600	37%
5. Fine and Applied Arts	25,800	37%
6. Letters (English, etc.)	24,100	41%
7. Health Professions (except Nursing)	21,900	30%
8. Public Affairs and Services	20,700	45%
9. Home Economics	17,500	5%
10. Sociology	12,600	33%
11. Foreign Languages	8,400	24%

BACHELOR'S DEGREES CONFERRED ON WOMEN:
Total in Eleven Popular Fields Listed 265,300
Total in All Fields 455,800

Eleven Fields as a Percentage of All Fields = 58.2%

Field of Study	Popularity for Men (Number of Degrees Conferred on Men)	Gender Gap (Percent in Field Conferred on Women)
POPULAR MAJORS TAKEN MAINLY BY MEN:		
1. Business and Management (except Accounting)	96,700	33%
2. Engineering	62,500	9%
3. Accounting	27,300	36%
4. Biological Sciences	26,800	42%
5. Physical Sciences	17,900	24%
6. Political Science and Government	16,300	36%
7. Agriculture	16,000	30%
8. Economics	12,500	30%
9. History	12,100	37%
10. Computer and Information Sciences	7,800	30%
11. Mathematical Subjects	6,600	42%

Table 4-4 Popular College Majors among Men and Women College Graduates in 1980 (*continued*)

BACHELOR'S DEGREES CONFERRED ON MEN:

Total in Eleven Popular Fields Listed 302,500

Total in All Fields 473,600

Eleven Fields as a Percentage of All Fields = 63.9%

TOTAL DEGREES CONFERRED ON BOTH SEXES 929,400

Source: Calculated from United States Bureau of the Census, *Statistical Abstract of the United States:* 1982–83, Table 278, p. 167.

rewards"—the work itself is rewarding. Work values favoring income, security, and prestige, on the other hand, result in jobs yielding "extrinsic rewards"—the outside rewards produced by the job are more important than the work itself. After surveying a national sample of over 9000 young adults in 1979, sociologists Paul Lindsay and William E. Knox reported that most women preferred a job where the work itself is rewarding (intrinsic rewards), while most men gave greater importance to the outside rewards the work produces (extrinsic rewards).

These gender differences in occupational values contribute to the extreme sexual stereotyping found in four fields—home economics, nursing, engineering, and elementary education. The women's fields all involve interpersonal relations and altruism, while the men's field—engineering—does not (Table 4-3). Engineering, on the other hand, consistently leads to much higher earnings than does home economics, nursing, or elementary education.

Sexual stereotyping also could be said to exist in fields in which, say, seventy percent or more of all undergraduate majors are of the same gender. For men these are bachelor's degrees in the physical sciences, economics, agriculture, and computer science. For women they are four-year degrees in foreign languages, the health professions, and secondary education.

You may share my belief that occupational choices should result from one's individual interests, talents, and goals, and not from the sexual stereotyping of occupations. If so, then you may agree that a wise occupational choice involves an open questioning of what it is you want from a job. At this point we can add gender to our earlier discussion about the consistency, or lack of it, between your occupational values and the requirements of your chosen career.

If your occupational values match the job requirements of your chosen field, then you are making a consistent choice. And if your desired occupation happens to be one dominated by your own sex, then your interests also coincide with what many people expect of your gender. You have a three-way consistency.

Sometimes a consistent occupational choice leads to a field dominated by members of the opposite sex. Extreme examples would be men wanting to become nurses (an attractive field, as we have seen), or women wanting to become engineers (also a large and growing occupation). If this is your situation, you should do well given the consistency between what you want from a job and what the work requires. But because of the inconsistency between your gender and that of most people in your occupation, you may experience gender-related problems on the job. You can expect your behavior to generate increased social pressures to stop what you are doing and to conform to the social norm instead.

In spite of pressures for gender conformity, the work you choose is for you alone to decide. It is a matter of how much your occupational values mean to you, and how willing you are to resist social pressures in order to achieve your values. If you want to learn more about the experiences of others who choose to cross the gender line, as a start you may wish to read the August 1982 issue of the journal, *Work and Occupations.* That issue includes articles about the social situation of female autoworkers, women lawyers, and male strippers.

A third possibility is that you are making an inconsistent occupational choice, and your gender is the cause of the problem. Here you are choosing an occupation based on what you think people expect of your sex, but you really would prefer some other line of work. Your gender conforms to the job so you can expect few, if any, gender-related job problems. But your inconsistent occupational choice increases the likelihood that you will not like the work itself. And if you dislike a job, chances are you will not do your best in it. You may eventually decide to leave the field—even after having invested your college education preparing for it and having spent valuable years at the start of your career working in it—for a more compatible occupation.

Today more women than men are crossing the occupational gender line. The sexual stereotyping of many occupations is eroding as people become increasingly willing to receive more women in occupations traditionally dominated by men. Sociologist Lloyd B. Lueptow reports that among high-school seniors more females were choosing traditionally male white-collar occupations in the early 1970s than they had chosen in the mid–1960s. But occupations dominated by females, and male blue-collar occupations, were as strongly sex-typed among high-school seniors in 1975 as they had been in 1964.

The movement of women into traditionally male white-collar occupations shows up in our list of popular college majors. In 1980 forty-two percent of mathematics majors were women, and over one-third of accounting bachelor's degrees were conferred on women. Women accounted for thirty percent or more of all four-year degrees granted in such fields as business and management, economics, and computer and information sciences. But only a few men had yet begun taking four-year college degrees in, for example, home economics or nursing.

With an increasingly wide range of attractive occupations opening for college-graduate women, many more women are deciding to combine the role of full-time worker with that of wife. How numerous are employed wives? How do couples gain when wives work outside the home?

HOW MANY EMPLOYED WIVES?

In the not-too-distant past, most wives did not work outside the home. In 1950, for example, three-quarters of wives living with their husbands were not in the labor force. Social expectations in the 1950s assumed a division of labor between husband and wife. The husband was responsible for being the breadwinner and for financially supporting the family, while the wife was responsible for home and family life. At that time married women could seek paid employment if they wanted (whether full or part time), but most chose to be full-time wives and mothers.

The women most likely to be in the labor force, both in the 1950s and in the 1980s, were and are those without husbands. Social values about them have remained unchanged—unmarried women, like men, were and are expected to work to support themselves. Most did, and most still do— between sixty to eighty percent, depending on age.

The greatest change in women's employment over the last thirty years involved working wives. In most families in the United States today, working wives are the rule and not the exception. Sixty percent of wives between the ages of twenty and forty-four were working in 1980, almost double the proportion working in 1960.

The women least likely to work were and are young wives with children less than six years old. By 1980, however, the presence of young children had become a less important factor in a wife's decision to work outside the home. Among wives living with their husbands in 1960, only one-fifth with children under six years old were in the labor force. By 1980, almost half of them were.

Changes in men's—as well as women's—values about wives working accompanied the growing numbers of working wives. When a wife goes to work, a husband loses a full-time person in the home. And if the couple has any children still at home, the family also loses a full-time mother for the children. Sociologists Ronald C. Kessler and James A. McRae, Jr. have documented that psychological distress is greater among married men whose wives work outside the home than among husbands whose wives are full-time homemakers. If husbands pay a psychological cost for having working wives, what do couples gain?

A working wife can gain in self-esteem by accomplishing her occupational goals. A couple in which both spouses are employed may share more mutual interests and communicate better with each other. And then there is the matter of having two incomes. Two jobs provide greater resilience against the possibility of either spouse becoming unemployed. Working couples, on the average, also have access to higher family incomes. In 1980, couples with working wives had average incomes forty-two percent higher than couples in which the wife stayed home—$26,900 compared with $19,000.

A more subtle gain for the husband was a change in the traditional division of labor between husband and wife. By contributing to the family's income, a working wife relieves her husband of the sole responsibility for supporting the family. The additional income she earns can reduce the career and income pressures that he otherwise would feel. He could work in a less demanding occupation or be less competitive for pay raises in his chosen field. It is perhaps more than just a coincidence that the proportion of women holding two or more jobs increased from two to four percent during the 1970s, while the figure for men declined slightly from seven to less than six percent. Sociologists Joan Huber and Glenna Spitze suggest that, should he choose to do so, a husband with a working wife could devote less time and effort to the work-a-day world, and more to his private interests—including undertaking a more active role in homemaking and child care.

In the traditional division of labor between husband and wife, many women took a man's potential for success in a career and for earning a good income—as well as his personality, looks, and values—into account when judging what kind of husband he would make. Yet few men in the 1950s and 1960s gave much thought to their wives' earning potential or future occupational status. With the increasing acceptance of wives working, however, some men began considering a woman's earning power in addition to her interests and abilities for being a wife, mother, and homemaker. And some women who intended to have careers began assessing their prospective mates not only for their occupational potential but also for their attitudes about egalitarianism and about sharing household and childrearing responsibilities.

This shift in values is an example of the growing social pressures on many young women that led them to believe that they had little choice but to enter and successfully compete in the labor force. More women accepted the value that paid employment is important for self-fulfillment. More young women also came to believe in the value of being self-supporting—a belief that grew with the increase, over the past twenty years, in the number of divorced women who had to work to support themselves. With the higher incidence of divorce, some women came to believe that full-time employment during marriage was a wise thing to do. It gave them greater financial independence both within the marriage and afterwards (should the marriage dissolve through divorce). The upshot was that paid employment became much more attractive to women by the 1980s than it had been back in the 1950s and early 1960s.

WHO WILL BE WORKING IN 1995?

During the last twenty-five years two great changes in attitudes about working have occurred in the United States. The first involved the movement of most younger women out of the home and into the labor force. As recently as 1960, for example, less than half of the women in their early twenties were employed or looking for a job. By 1981, the figure had risen to seventy percent. The second change was the growth of early retirement among older workers. One-third of men sixty-five and over were still working or seeking work in 1960, but less than one-fifth were by 1981. As a result of these trends, today most men and women between the ages of twenty and sixty are in the labor force (at work or seeking work), while few people over sixty-five are still employed.

What of the near future? The United States Department of Labor assumes these trends will continue at least through the mid–1990s. Higher proportions of women, and smaller proportions of older people, will be working. By 1995 about seven-eighths of all white men and women in their early twenties will be in the labor force. Among blacks of the same age, the Department of Labor expects at least three-quarters of men and at least two-thirds of women to be working or seeking work. If these projections come to pass, the United States labor force in 1995 would be composed mainly of people born between 1935 and 1975. By figuring how old you will be in 1995, you can find your place in the picture I have drawn of the labor force in that year (Figure 4-1).

People born in 1968, for example, will be twenty-seven years old in 1995. The great majority, regardless of gender or marital status, will be working. Among the men in that cohort, ninety-four percent probably will be in the labor force. Most of those not working will be either still in school, or unable to work because of a disability. Eighty-four percent of all women in their late twenties or early thirties probably will be working outside the home. (In 1980, two-thirds of women at that stage in life were in the labor force; back in 1970, fewer than half were.)

Perhaps the most striking feature of the 1995 projection is the shrinking number of younger workers. The change will be caused by the smaller cohorts of people born in the late 1960s and succeeding years, gradually replacing the large Baby Boom cohort. With fewer people competing for beginning jobs, it seems reasonable to assume that:

1. The youth unemployment problem will be less.
2. Younger members of racial or ethnic minority groups will have better employment opportunities.

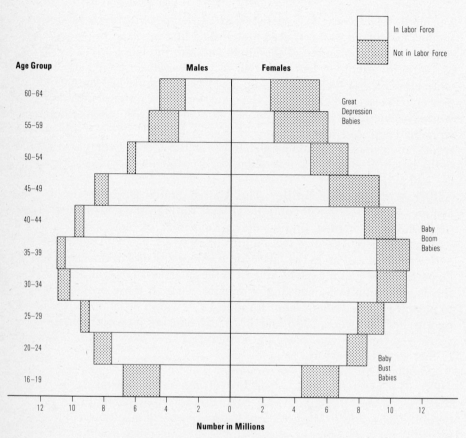

FIGURE 4-1 WHO WILL BE WORKING OR SEEKING WORK IN 1995? Total and Labor Force Populations by Gender among People Sixteen through Sixty-Four Years Old, United States, 1995

Source: U.S. Bureau of the Census, *Current Population Reports,* Series P-25, No. 922 (October 1982); U.S. Bureau of Labor Statistics, *Monthly Labor Review* (December 1980).

3. Pay raises will be larger, and promotions faster, for workers born after 1965 than for those born between 1945 and 1960—other things being equal.
4. Older workers (those born before 1940) willing to do entry-level work will have opportunities for retraining and employment.
5. More robots will be used for work previously done by young, beginning, unskilled, and semiskilled workers.

The 1995 projections assume that most people between twenty and forty-five will have little choice about working—they will be under great social pressures to be employed. These pressures begin to relax, however, for women after age forty-five, and for men after their mid-fifties. After those ages, increasing numbers leave the labor force—some involuntarily. By 1995 those not in the labor force may account for as many as one-third or more of all women in their late forties and early fifties, and one-third of all men in their late fifties and early sixties. The trend toward early retirement could result in as few as one-ninth of men, and one-fifteenth of women, continuing to work after age sixty-five.

The earlier retirement age of women once again reflects the important connection for women between marital status and labor force status. As we have seen, women without husbands, and men generally, are expected to work full time to support themselves and their families. But because of the value many people place on wife, mother, and homemaker roles, they accept the idea of married women working part time, interrupting their work history, or retiring at an early age. All three options are made possible for wives by husbands contributing to the financial support of the household.

And that brings us to a major life choice that none of us can avoid—whether to be married or unmarried. The pros and cons of each are the topic of the following chapter.

5/

Married or Unmarried?

Whatever you choose to do regarding marriage, you will find social pressures to marry (or remarry) most intense at certain ages—late teens through late twenties for women, and early twenties through early thirties for men. You can better deal with these expectations when you know how marriage and divorce trends are changing, what your agemates will be doing, and why people marry or not.

Recent trends tell us that if you want to delay or reject marriage, you will have substantial company. While most people eventually marry, the minority that does not is increasing. One-fifth of all people eighteen years old and over in 1982 had never married, up from one-seventh in 1965. Those who marry are doing so at later ages. By 1980 the median age at first marriage had increased to 23.6 years for men, and to 21.8 years for women.

Divorce rates are at historically high levels. The 1980 divorce rate was more than double that of 1965. If current divorce rates continue, about half of recent marriages eventually will end in divorce. And of those who do divorce, fewer are remarrying. The remarriage rate of divorced women aged twenty-five through forty-four years declined by one-third between 1970 and 1980. The comparable remarriage rate among divorced men dropped even more (by forty-two percent). With more divorces and fewer remarriages, the proportion divorced and not remarried among all adults in the United States more than doubled between 1965 and 1981 (to seven percent).

I am not advocating being unmarried, but simply reporting that pressures to marry are reducing as the acceptance of being single increases. (By "single" I mean not only being never-married, but also being divorced or widowed and not remarried.) Some people are happier being married, some prefer being single. The choice can be made today with greater freedom from intense social pressures for being married such as those that prevailed in the 1950s and 1960s.

It should be noted that older women have less choice than do older men about being married because the number of men declines more rapidly with age. After age thirty-five there are not enough never-married, divorced, and widowed men to marry all of the unmarried women even if all of these men married. But for people who want to be unmarried, the number of people of the opposite sex is of little concern. Assuming they can support themselves, everybody has the same opportunity to be unmarried.

The purpose of this chapter is to help you think about being married or unmarried. The projected marriage choices of your agemates will be described, as will those of other cohorts. Widely held values regarding marriage and nonmarriage will be discussed. Specifically, this chapter covers:

1. The proportions of your cohort projected to be never-married, married, divorced, or widowed in 1995.
2. A sociological explanation of why most people marry.
3. Marriage values and single values.
4. Recent trends in sexual ideologies.
5. Being unmarried; being married.

MARITAL STATUS PROJECTIONS FOR 1995

You may want to ask yourself in which marital category you expect to be in ten or fifteen years. If you are not yet married, how long do you plan to postpone marriage? Indefinitely? If you currently are married, would you remarry if widowed or divorced? Just because most people over thirty are currently married does not mean that you also have to be—unless you choose to be. In making that choice, it helps to have precise knowledge about the proportions of your cohort that are expected to be single, married (or remarried), divorced, or widowed. Knowing how many people in your cohort will be married or single in the near future may help you resist social pressures for or against marriage in the meantime.

Because age is linked with marital status, your cohort's marriage choices can be projected into the future. We don't have to make our own projections of marital status by age and sex, because the United States Social Security Administration has done it for us. They have made projections of future marital status to use in estimating their future financial commitments. You can use their projections to gain some insight into your own life.

The Social Security projections ask: "What proportions of each cohort will be never-married, married, divorced, or widowed in the future if recent marriage, divorce, and mortality rates continue?" The projections were made for the total population covered by Social Security and thus include some people living outside the fifty States and the District of Columbia. No separate projections were made for whites, blacks, or Hispanics.

I selected the marital status projections for 1995 because people born around 1968 will be in their late twenties at that time and thus several years beyond the average age at first marriage (Figure 5-1). The diagram also shows the marital status of all other cohorts in 1995—of persons born from before 1900 through those born in 1995.

The links between age, gender, and marital status show up clearly in Figure 5-1. Most people under twenty-five, particularly men, will not yet have married. Currently divorced people will be found mainly among people between the ages of thirty and fifty, especially women. Almost everyone will have married at some time in their lives before reaching their early fifties, and most middle-aged people will be then currently married. Widowhood becomes increasingly frequent among women from middle age onward, while most older men will be married (or remarried).

Once you find your own cohort in Figure 5-1, you can see how the members of your sex and cohort probably will have made their marriage choices by 1995. To aid you in comparing your cohort with others, I will detail the situations of four cohorts twenty years apart in age. (Your own cohort may be one of the four—if not, Figure 5-1 will show you how your cohort is like or unlike the four discussed.) There are two important reasons for learning about cohorts other than your own. First, descriptions of cohorts older than you can give you some idea of what to expect when you reach that stage in life. Second, the information about other cohorts can give you added insight into the situations of relatives or friends who are either older or younger than you.

The balance of this section describes what marital patterns are expected in the near future, and how sex ratios and mortality influence marital status. The more general reasons why people marry or not will be examined in the last part of this chapter. One other point: for the sake of clarity, I use the word "will" to describe the 1995 marital status projections—but they "will" materialize only if the assumptions on which they are based turn out to be true.

The 1966-70 Birth Cohort

The late 1960s babies will be in their late twenties in 1995. The sex ratio among single people will favor women—there will be five men for every four women among unmarried people in their late twenties. This figure actually understates the men available to young women to marry because young women not only marry men of their own age, but they also marry men older than themselves.

The excess number of unmarried men among younger adults results from men generally postponing marriage longer than women. Two-fifths of men

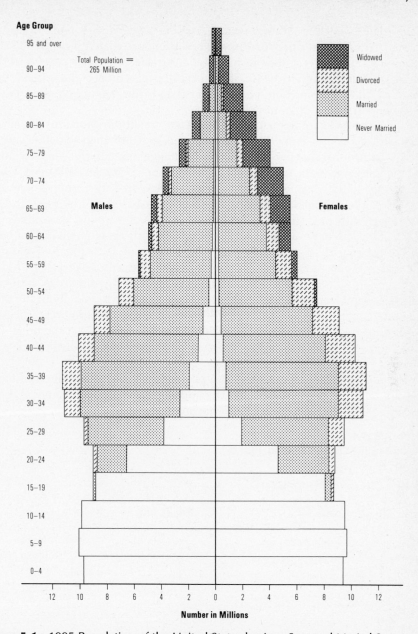

Figure 5-1 1995 Population of the United States by Age, Sex, and Marital Status.

Source: J. F. Faber and J. C. Wilkin, "Social Security Area Population Projections, 1981," Actuarial Study No. 85, Social Security Administration (July 1981), SSA Pub. No. 11-11532, Table 20D.

in their late twenties, and one-fifth of women the same age, will have never married. The women's proportion will be little more than it was in 1980. But the men's represents a sizable increase from the one-third never-married among men of this age in 1980. Should these projections come to pass, they would result in grooms being even older than brides among couples marrying for the first time than now is the case.

Given the increase in postponed marriage, smaller proportions of people, especially men, are expected to be married in 1995 than was the case in 1980. The proportion currently married among all men in their late twenties will decline from sixty-two to fifty-three percent between 1980 and 1995. The change will be less for women—from seventy to sixty-eight percent. For both sexes the proportions divorced and not remarried will increase.

You can interpret these figures in two ways. As I have just described, you can examine the percentages and see what proportions of a cohort will be in each of the marital status categories. The other way is to speak of the percentages in terms of the odds for which marital status is most or least likely. Even though you cannot predict with certainty your own marital status ten or fifteen years from now, nevertheless it is reasonable to talk about the odds that someone of your age and sex will be single, married, divorced, or widowed. Your own situation may be exceptional—you may beat the odds. But chances are the odds will apply to many of your friends and relatives your own age.

To help you think about the 1995 projections from either point of view, here are both the percentages, and the odds, of men and women in the 1966-70 birth cohort being in one or another marital status:

1966–70 Cohort (Age 25–29 in 1995)

	Women	Men
Then Currently Married	68% (1 in 1.5)	53% (1 in 2)
Never Married	20% (1 in 5)	40% (1 in 2.5)
Divorced & Not Remarried	12% (1 in 8)	7% (1 in 14)
Widowed & Not Remarried	** (1 in 470)	** (Almost None)
Total	100%	100%

** = Less than 1 percent.

The 1946-50 Birth Cohort

People born in the late 1940s will be in their late forties in 1995. They can expect that about three-fourths of both the men and the women in their cohort will be then currently married (including remarried persons).

Avoiding a first marriage will be more characteristic of men than women. Almost twice the proportion of never-married men than women will still be postponing marriage—nine percent compared with five percent respectively. These men will be remaining unmarried in spite of a sex ratio among single people that favors them. Among unmarried people in their late forties in 1995, there will be five women for every four men. This figure actually understates the availability of unmarried women for men in their late forties, because older men not only marry women of their same age, they also marry younger women.

Even though never-married, middle-aged men persist in postponing marriage longer than women, divorced middle-aged men remarry more readily than do divorced women. In this case, the sex ratio (just described) among middle-aged single people gives divorced or widowed men more choice about remarrying than previously married women have. The same number of men as women will have divorced, of course, but the higher male remarriage rate results in a smaller proportion of men who remain divorced. One-eighth of all men in their late forties will have been divorced and not remarried in 1995. The comparable figure for women will be one-fifth divorced and not remarried. The percentages and odds expected for this Baby Boom cohort are:

1946–50 Cohort (Age 45–49 in 1995)

	Women	Men
Then Currently Married	72% (1 in 1.4)	78% (1 in 1.3)
Divorced & Not Remarried	21% (1 in 5)	12% (1 in 8)
Never Married	5% (1 in 22)	9% (1 in 10)
Widowed & Not Remarried	2% (1 in 53)	** (1 in 178)
Total	100%	100%

** = Less than 1 percent.

The 1926-30 Birth Cohort

You may know some friends or relatives who will be in their late sixties in 1995. Chances are they will be married and living with their spouses—over half of the women and four-fifths of the men. The smaller fraction of then currently married women is explained by the women who will not have remarried after widowhood (one-quarter) or divorce (one-eighth).

Given the cumulative importance of male mortality by this stage in life, there will be twice as many widows as divorcees among women in their late sixties in 1995. The greater male mortality also produces a large deficit of unmarried men. In 1995 there will be only two unmarried men for every five unmarried women among people in their late sixties. Thus the opportunity for remarriage will be much greater for older men than women.

1926–30 Cohort (Age 65–69 in 1995)

	Women	Men
Then Currently Married	58% (1 in 1.7)	79% (1 in 1.3)
Widowed & Not Remarried	26% (1 in 4)	7% (1 in 15)
Divorced & Not Remarried	12% (1 in 8)	8% (1 in 12)
Never Married	4% (1 in 24)	6% (1 in 16)
Total	100%	100%

The 1906-10 Birth Cohort

The marital situation of people in their late eighties reveals how important are the twin forces of greater rates of male mortality and male remarriage. Your own expected longevity will be discussed in Chapter Eight. At this point, suffice to say that your chances for living into your eighties are reasonably good if you are a woman, but not so good if you are a man. If you do live into your late eighties, chances are you will be widowed if you are a woman, and still married (including remarried) if you are a man. The figures expected for 1995, for example, are that: (1) three-quarters of all women in their late eighties will be widowed and not remarried; and (2) over half of the men the same age will be married (or remarried) and living with their spouses.

There will be only one unmarried man in his late eighties for every five single women of the same age. For both genders the proportions of never-married, or divorced and not remarried, will be small:

1906–10 Cohort (Age 85–89 in 1995)

	Women	Men
Widowed & Not Remarried	75% (1 in 1.3)	34% (1 in 3)
Then Currently Married	14% (1 in 7)	56% (1 in 2)
Never Married	6% (1 in 16)	5% (1 in 20)
Divorced & Not Remarried	5% (1 in 20)	5% (1 in 20)
Total	100%	100%

A QUESTION OF VALUES

Marital status projections tell us what we can reasonably expect for each of our cohorts in 1995. But they do not tell us why people will be making the choices that they do. As we have seen, men generally postpone marriage longer when they are young, but are more likely to remarry if divorced or widowed. Women, in contrast, marry earlier but are less likely than men to remarry after their late twenties (in part due to sex-ratio imbalances). Does the earlier marriage of women mean that younger women benefit more than younger men from marriage?And then, among middle-aged and older people, does the higher male remarriage rate mean that older men benefit more than older women from being married? Could it be that men hold different values about marriage than women do?

If being married is the behavior expected of almost all of us, then what does the high divorce rate mean? One-fifth of women, and one-ninth of men, between the ages of thirty-five and fifty-four are projected to be divorced and not remarried in 1995. Yet few plan to divorce when they marry. Can so many millions be making such an important mistake in choosing a spouse?

For answers to such questions, we must ask: Why do people marry? Why do they remain married? The sociological assumption is that although marriage is a matter of choice, it is a decision shaped by the society in which people live. Marriage helps individuals, and the society, achieve certain goals. With the knowledge we have gained so far in this chapter about the ages at which marriage choices are made, let us consider why people choose to marry, divorce, or remarry.

MARRIAGE VALUES AND SINGLE VALUES

Do you believe most people choose randomly to marry and to remain married? Is it simply a matter of "love at first sight"? Is divorce only a matter of "bad luck"? If so, then chance alone determines when to marry, with whom, and for how long. In effect, marriage becomes inexplicable both to the people involved and to others.

Sociologists make a less glib assumption. They believe most, though not all, people make their marriage decisions according to their social values—that people may love with their hearts, but they marry with their heads. You can understand why people choose to be married or single once you understand what they expect from marriage based on their values. From this perspective, a high divorce rate would mean that many people have good reasons for marrying at one stage in life only to decide five, fifteen, or twenty-five years later that they then have other good reasons for not being married.

Probably all of us know a couple that married while both were still in their teens, for example, because they loved each other and for no other reason. If asked, they might explain that their spouse was their chief, and perhaps only, source of intimacy and affection. What are the chances that a couple that marries for just this one reason will remain married to each other throughout their lives?

Generally speaking, long-term prospects are not good for a marriage based only on feelings of mutual affection. If either wife or husband has a change of heart, grows bored with, or comes actively to dislike the other, then the sole reason for being married will be lost. Having had a good reason for marriage, that person would now argue a persuasive reason for divorce: that no mistake was made in marrying as both loved each other at that time, but it would be a mistake at this time to remain married now that mutual feelings of love no longer exist.

If they had other reasons for being married, however, they may choose to remain married even if their strong feelings of affection for each other cool. A pragmatic sociological assumption is that the more benefits a marriage provides, the more highly motivated a person is to maintain it. Our present interest is in spelling out some of the ideal benefits that motivate people to marry and to remain married. These desired ideals for being married can be thought of as "marriage values."

Similarly, "single values" can be thought of as the desired ideals for being unmarried. As stated above, the term "single" refers here not only to being never-married, but also to being divorced or widowed and not remarried. People who are unmarried by choice may differ in which particular set of single values they hold. Some may prefer a single life to the responsibilities, sharing, and reduced privacy of being married. Others, who are divorced or widowed, may choose not to remarry because they already have achieved certain marriage values (such as parenthood) through their previous marriage. Some may not remarry because their previous marriage did not give them the marriage values they had expected. Having been burned once, they are twice shy. By default, single values become more attractive.

Seven widely held "marriage values," and seven corresponding "single values," are listed in Questionnaire B. The purpose of the questionnaire is simply to help you sort out your own values regarding marriage. It is no substitute, of course, for the detailed personal surveys used by marriage and family researchers and counselors. All of the fourteen values listed should be self-explanatory. At first glance, "sexual variety" and "freedom from expectations to be sexually active" may seem out of place on the same list. But being single appeals both to those who desire sexual variety, and to those who wish to abstain from sex.

The questionnaire is oversimplified in listing only some of the many values connected with being married or single. In spite of its informality, it does serve to show you whether you desire to be married (or single) for just one or two reasons, or for a whole set of motives. The more reasons you have for being married (or single), the more likely you are to maintain that status even if you do not succeed in realizing all of your desires.

In addition to filling it out yourself, you may want to make a copy and ask your spouse, or prospective mate, also to complete it. You do not need to share the same set of marriage values to have a stable marriage. But at least you should each have an idea of the current reasons you both are in, or are planning, the same marriage. The more reasons you each have for being married, and the more strongly you each feel about them, the greater the chances are that your marriage will endure.

A high score in either marriage or single categories is less important than the difference between your scores. The difference indicates how committed you are to one or the other marriage option. The larger the difference between your two scores, the more strongly you are expressing the values of one marital condition as opposed to the other. A small difference, say five points or less, indicates ambivalence. You either want the best of both worlds, or neither one. But you cannot be both married and single at the same time—you must make a choice. You can postpone your decision, however, until you make up your mind—postponing marriage if you are single, or postponing divorce if you are married.

SEXUAL IDEOLOGIES

Sexual desires, or the lack of them, are involved in four of the fourteen marriage and single values—sexual fidelity, sexual legitimization, variety, or abstinence. If you value sexual fidelity and sexual legitimization, for example, you would prefer marriage to a more informal sexual relationship such as just living together. Ideally, marriage eliminates sexual competition from others for your sexual partner. You expect marriage to bring with it a spoken promise from your spouse to "forsake all others," and an unspoken understanding from others that they will honor your marriage bonds.

Does the earlier marriage of women mean that more young women than young men highly value sexual fidelity and legitimized sexual activity? Is the answer to this question a matter of biology or of sociology? From a sociological viewpoint, our sexual behavior is primarily determined by what we have come to believe is socially desirable or undesirable. Physical and hormonal differences between the sexes exist, of course. But individual differences within each sex, and widely different sex roles in various cultures, weaken the logic of a purely biological answer regarding which sex prefers fidelity or sexual legitimization. As the family sociologist, Ira L. Reiss, expressed the matter:

> The debate about genetic differences . . . really has very little to do with unalterable gender-role differences or sexual-drive differences. Learning is so powerful a force in the human situation that such average tendencies do not necessarily predetermine very much at all. Our ideologies will determine our gender roles and our sexuality far more than our hormonal differences (Reiss, 1981, Page 273).

QUESTIONNAIRE B: **Personal Questionnaire about Ideal Standards for Being Married or Unmarried**

Procedure: Place a checkmark to indicate whether, and how strongly, you desire or reject a given value. Add up your checkmarks in each column, and multiply them by one to five points depending on how strongly you feel about each. By adding these figures together, you obtain your total MARRIAGE SCORE or SINGLE SCORE.

	Strongly Reject				Strongly Desire
	1	2	3	4	5
MARRIAGE VALUES					
1. Sexual Fidelity	____	____	____	____	____
2. Legitimized Sexual Activity	____	____	____	____	____
3. Parenthood	____	____	____	____	____
4. Sharing A Home	____	____	____	____	____
5. Being Depended On and Being Dependent	____	____	____	____	____
6. Sharing Income, Resources, Skills	____	____	____	____	____
7. Long-term, Stable Companionship	____	____	____	____	____
Total Checkmarks	____	____	____	____	____
Multiply by:	× 1	× 2	× 3	× 4	× 5
Subtotals	____	____	____	____	____

Total MARRIAGE SCORE = _____ (Add five subtotals together)

(Continued on following page.)

Assuming this is so, it follows that sexual ideologies can change over time, creating differences between cohorts in sexual attitudes and behavior. What are the prevailing sexual ideologies in the United States today? Reiss outlines two—the "Traditional-Romantic" and the "Modern-Naturalistic." The Traditional-Romantic ideology is based on a double standard with males being dominant. Sexuality without affection (body-centered sexuality) is held in low esteem, but much more so for women than for men. This is so because men are believed to be driven by more powerful sexual forces than women.

(Questionnaire B Continued.)

	Strongly Reject				Strongly Desire
	1	2	3	4	5

SINGLE VALUES

1. Sexual Variety

2. Freedom from Expectations to Be Sexually Active

3. Freedom from Parental Responsibilities

4. Job and Career Goals

5. Personal Independence

6. Spending Your Income on Yourself

7. Personal Privacy

Total Checkmarks					
Multiply by:	× 1	× 2	× 3	× 4	× 5
Subtotals					

Total SINGLE SCORE = _____ (Add five subtotals together)

From your: MARRIAGE SCORE   _____
SUBTRACT your: SINGLE SCORE   − _____
Difference (plus or minus)   = _____

A virtuous woman avoids men who cannot control their sexual drives. Men may seek heterosexual coitus without becoming emotionally involved, while women's sexual interests are proper only when redeemed by the power of romantic love.

The Modern-Naturalistic ideology, in contrast, is based on egalitarian relations between females and males. Body-centered sexuality is thought to have positive value for both sexes, but it is held in lower esteem than sexuality involving affection. Sexual drives are strong for both men and women, but manageable by both as are other basic emotional forces. Heterosexual coitus is believed to be only one of many acceptable ways of physically expressing sexuality. Guilt is associated with sexuality only when force or fraud is involved.

QUESTIONNAIRE C: **Personal Questionnaire about Sexual Ideologies**

	Strongly Disagree				*Strongly Agree*
	1	2	3	4	5

TRADITIONAL VALUES

1. Sex roles should be distinct but interdependent, with men dominating. ___ ___ ___ ___ ___

2. Sexuality without affection should be avoided by women. ___ ___ ___ ___ ___

3. Sexuality is a powerful, unmanageable emotion for men. ___ ___ ___ ___ ___

4. The main sexual objective should be heterosexual coitus. ___ ___ ___ ___ ___

5. Love alone redeems sexuality from any guilt for women. ___ ___ ___ ___ ___

	1	2	3	4	5
Total Checkmarks	___	___	___	___	___
Multiply by:	× 1	× 2	× 3	× 4	× 5
Subtotals	___	___	___	___	___

Total TRADITIONAL SCORE = _____ (Add five subtotals together)

(Continued on following page.)

You may agree with some parts of each ideology, or you may strongly favor only one. Filling out a simple questionnaire may help you recognize which sexual values you hold, and how strongly you feel about them (Questionnaire C). By considering your stand on each value item, you may become more fully aware of your own sexual ideology and how it developed through your upbringing and experiences. For the sake of brevity, I shall refer to the "Traditional-Romantic" ideology as "Traditional," and the "Modern-Naturalistic" as "Naturalistic."

A large difference between your scores for the two sexual ideologies indicates a strong commitment. A small difference, say five points or less, reflects ambivalence—indecision over whether you believe men and women are sexually similar, or whether you believe they are sexually distinct, with males having a stronger sexual drive. As with the questionnaire for marriage and single values, you also may want to ask your spouse, or potential spouse, to complete the sexual ideology questionnaire, and then compare it with yours.

(Questionnaire C Continued.)

	Strongly Disagree				Strongly Agree
	1	2	3	4	5

NATURALISTIC VALUES

1. Sex roles should be similar and promote equality ____ ____ ____ ____ ____
2. While of less worth than sexuality with affection, sexuality without affection still has positive value for both sexes ____ ____ ____ ____ ____
3. Sexual feelings are manageable, as other basic emotions are ____ ____ ____ ____ ____
4. The main sexual objective should be physical and psychological intimacy ____ ____ ____ ____ ____
5. A variety of sexual acts should be accepted without guilt by both genders providing force or fraud is not involved ____ ____ ____ ____ ____

Total Checkmarks ____ ____ ____ ____ ____

Multiply by: × 1 × 2 × 3 × 4 × 5

Subtotals ____ ____ ____ ____ ____

Total NATURALISTIC SCORE = ____ (Add five subtotals together)

From your: TRADITIONAL SCORE ____
SUBTRACT your: NATURALISTIC SCORE − ____
Difference = ____

SOURCE: Adapted from Ira L. Reiss, "Some Observations on Ideology and Sexuality in America," *Journal of Marriage and the Family* (May 1981), pp. 279–281.

RECENT TRENDS IN SEXUAL IDEOLOGIES

Assuming that personal sexual ideologies shape marriage choices, the question remains: Which sexual ideology generally favors sexual fidelity and sexual legitimization—the Traditional or the Naturalistic? The answer depends, in part, on which gender is involved. Among traditionalists, the double standard allows unmarried men sexual variety—a license to "sow wild oats." But because romantic love must exist before a woman can become sexually involved, she is not allowed a variety of sexual partners. She is raised to believe strongly in the value of sexual fidelity and legitimized sexual activity.

For traditional women believing in sexual fidelity and legitimacy, marriage is the only socially accepted means for having sexual relations. Traditionally minded men, however, often favor sexual variety before marriage. The stage is set for a battle of wills among unmarried people holding traditional sexual values, with women seeking to resolve the pressure by marriage. In this way, early marriage based on sexual fidelity becomes much more attractive to traditional women than men.

While sexuality with affection is also preferred by people holding the naturalistic sexual ideology, they are more tolerant of both genders having sexual relations before marriage. This aspect of the naturalistic view apparently is gaining acceptance in the United States. According to the National Opinion Research Center (NORC) of the University of Chicago, one-third of all adult respondents in 1983 believed that it was "not wrong at all" for a man and a woman to have sex relations before marriage, up from one-quarter in 1973. Over the same ten years the proportion holding the more traditional view that premarital sex was "always wrong" declined from one-third to one-quarter.

An argument could be made that the change in sexual ideologies, along with improvements in birth control technology, increased the number of young women who believed they did not have to be married to be sexually active. The growth of the naturalistic ideology during the 1970s and early 1980s coincided with an increase in the number of unmarried couples who were living together. Between 1970 and 1981, the number of such couples more than tripled to almost two million. Demographer Graham B. Spanier reports that for some couples, cohabitation—two unrelated adults of the opposite sex sharing the same household—has become an extended period of courtship that eventually results in marriage.

Most Americans, whether traditional or naturalistic, believe that marriage partners should be sexually faithful to each other. The strength of this social norm in the United States remained essentially unchanged between 1973 and 1982, according to the National Opinion Research Center's surveys. Throughout that period, over two-thirds of all adults surveyed stated that it was "always wrong" for a married person to have sexual relations with someone other than the marriage partner. At the other extreme, only one-twenty-fifth of the respondents believed such behavior was "not wrong at all."

Given the double standard underlying the traditional view, however, husbands would have a greater chance of being unfaithful and then being accepted back by their wives than vice versa. The traditionally minded man would expect his wife to "understand" how he had lost control over his sexual urges. But if she were unfaithful, he would feel justified in being intolerant, unforgiving, and more likely to seek to end the marriage through divorce.

The increasing acceptance of the naturalistic point of view may help explain at least some of the increase in divorce. A wife holding naturalistic values would be less tolerant than a traditionally minded wife of her husband being unfaithful. She would expect her husband to keep his sexual emotions under control—to act responsibly toward her. A naturalistic woman would be as intolerant of marital infidelity as a naturalistic man. And if her paid employment in the labor force made divorce financially feasible, she might be as likely as her husband to seek divorce. From this perspective, the shift to a naturalistic ideology based on equality and mutual trust lessens the likelihood that either husband or wife would tolerate sexual unfaithfulness.

The remarriage rate would be higher for men than for women among people holding the traditional sexual ideology, other things being equal. From the traditional viewpoint, men are assumed to be more sexually active and women supposedly are better able to accept sexual abstinence. Thus for men holding such values, one of the major attractions of being married is the opportunity for socially approved, regular sexual activity. This element of marriage would be less attractive to a traditionally minded woman who, for example, exchanges sexual activity for companionship or security. She would tolerate the advances of a sexually active husband out of love or a sense of duty. But should she become divorced or widowed, presumably she would not seek to remarry just to regain the opportunity for an active sexual life.

Remarriage rates among people holding the naturalistic sexual ideology, in contrast, should be more nearly equal partly because both genders supposedly equally desire regular sexual activity. With the growth of the more egalitarian sexual ideology during the 1970s, one would expect a decline in the gender gap in remarriage rates. This would be especially the case for young adults. They not only would include more people with egalitarian beliefs, but also they are still at those ages where the scarcity of men has not yet developed.

And that is what happened. Both in 1970 and in 1980 the sex ratio was essentially unchanged among unmarried people in their late twenties (126 and 124 unmarried males per 100 unmarried females respectively). But during that decade the gender gap in the remarriage rate narrowed rapidly among people in their late twenties. In this age group in 1970, the remarriage rate was sixty-seven percent higher for men than for women; ten years later, the comparable rate was only twenty-six percent higher.

BEING UNMARRIED

Ten of the fourteen marriage and single values listed in Questionnaire B are concerned in differing degrees with two major spheres of life—family life or having a full-time job and being independent. Based on your responses to those items, you probably have a good idea of how strongly you value family life, or full-time employment and personal independence, or elements of both.

If you value personal independence and privacy more than family ties and sharing, you may not want people becoming involved in your life. You may consider their concern about what you are doing as unwanted interference. Nor would you welcome expectations to help care for others' needs if you feel you do not have sufficient time or material resources for your own interests. If you feel this way, remaining (or becoming) single is attractive because it simplifies life by reducing expectations, social complexities, and potential sources of interpersonal stress.

If you have unfulfilled educational or career goals, the time commitments and income sharing expected in marriage are especially unattractive. The fewer family obligations of an unmarried person create more available time for study or a career. Keeping all your income for yourself helps you better afford the costs of higher education, or allows you the opportunity of taking an initially lower-paying job with good long-range prospects. Although commuter marriages with spouses living in different towns are becoming more frequent, single people generally are freer to move geographically, and thus can take advantage of a wider choice of schools or jobs than those available locally.

Living an independent single life presupposes an adequate means of self-support. For most men and women of working age, this means full-time employment. In terms of income alone, it is generally easier for men to maintain a certain standard of living as unmarried persons than it is for women. As you may recall from Chapter Three, women generally earn less than men. Among year-round full-time workers in 1980, women's earnings were less than two-thirds as large as men's. This average figure obscures important differences by age, which would make it easier for younger than older women to live alone. College-educated younger women earn three-quarters as much as men their same age, while older women only earn one-half has much as men (see Table 3-4).

BEING MARRIED

Marriage ideally helps you achieve several goals—parenthood, having a home life, having someone to care for, having people who care for you, sharing financial resources, and companionship. You may believe that the ideal marriage is one that eventually includes having at least one child. If so, you share a widely held value. Among adults responding in national surveys taken in the 1970s and early 1980s by the National Opinion Research Center of the University of Chicago, ninety-eight percent said that the ideal family is one that includes children.

Should your values lead you to desire being married, chances are you will be choosing between two major forms of marriage arrangements widely followed in the United States today—the "traditional-tradeoff" or the "contemporary-cooperative."

The Traditional-Tradeoff Marriage

The division of labor in a traditional marriage places family responsibilities primarily with the wife, and job and career goals with the husband. He is expected to be the breadwinner; she is expected to be the homemaker. His role as provider for the family is a tradeoff for the wife's roles as cook and housekeeper, and child-care provider should there be children.

Finding a reliable and secure provider for herself and her children, should she have any, is a major attraction of marriage for a traditionally minded woman. She is brought up to seek a husband who is a "good catch." She cares more about a man's having established himself in a job or career than about his age, and thus she is willing to marry a man older than herself. A like-minded man would want to postpone marriage and the breadwinner role until he had fulfilled most, if not all, of his educational goals and had a good job.

The traditional marriage is assumed to be for life. If you favor this marriage arrangement, consider what the consequences of widowhood may be. If you are the husband and become widowed while still of working age, your chances for maintaining your living standard are good. You may have lost your wife but you have not lost your means of livelihood. Should you choose to remarry, the favorable (from a man's point of view) surplus of unmarried women after age thirty-five increases your chances for finding another wife.

But if you are the wife who becomes widowed in a traditional marriage, you lose both your husband and your means of support. You may have five broad means of maintaining yourself: (1) the income from accumulated savings, life insurance benefits, etc.; (2) money contributed by your other relatives, including your children should you have any; (3) income earned through your own employment; (4) government social welfare benefits; and (5) Social Security benefits.

With no recent full-time employment experience, your earning power in the marketplace would be lower than that of women your own age and education who had continued working full time after marriage. Given the scarcity of unmarried men after age thiry-five, you would have a more difficult time finding another husband during, say, your fifties than your twenties. For these reasons, widowhood often results in a greater decline in material living conditions for widows than for widowers.

The increase in divorce in recent decades has some of the same consequences for traditional marriages as widowhood did in the past. A divorced husband can more easily maintain his living standards and, should he choose, remarry. A wife who has not been employed full time outside the home is more likely to suffer a decline in living standards after divorce, and, because of the sex ratio, to be less likely to remarry after her early thirties even if she so desires. The difficulties faced by a displaced homemaker can be compounded when she also is reponsible for the rearing of the couple's children.

This inequity in consequences gives the advantage to men in traditional marriages. The husband's advantage in the past, however, was tempered by the fact that he normally would not seek to make his wife a widow. But the increasing social acceptability of divorce has widened the husband's advantage. If he is in some way dissatisfied with his marriage, he would suffer less from a divorce than would his wife.

The Contemporary-Cooperative Marriage

The balance of power is more equal in a marriage where both spouses are employed full time outside the home. This is especially so when the wife's employment is viewed by the couple as being as important as the husband's. Instead of a distinct division of labor between husband and wife, the contemporary-cooperative marriage is based on a sharing between equals. The husband is not expected to meet all the couple's material needs and desires. The wife is expected to make her contribution to the family's finances by working outside the home.

According to the National Opinion Research Center surveys, traditional views about wives not working weakened during the 1970s. The proportion of all adults who disapproved of a married woman earning money if she had a husband capable of supporting her, declined from one-third to less than one-quarter between 1972 and 1983. The acceptance of wives having paid employment is one of the more important value changes of the past three decades. As we saw in Chapter Four, the proportion of wives aged twenty-five through forty-four who work outside the home increased from one-third to almost two-thirds between 1960 and 1981.

If you are a woman who works (or plans to work) full-time outside the home after marriage, you are gaining two major advantages over a wife's role in the traditional-tradeoff marriage. You are (or will be) less dependent on your husband for financial support. Other things being equal, you would be better able to support yourself should you become divorced or widowed. You also benefit, as does your husband, from the larger total family income your earnings make possible.

Just as the contemporary-cooperative marriage relieves the husband of total responsibility for financially maintaining the family, it also ideally relieves the wife of total responsibility for cooking, housekeeping, and child care. However household duties are divided, a sense of "our work" is supposed to replace traditional attitudes about "women's work" and "men's work." But this has not happened so far in many marriages where the wife works outside the home. Sociologists Philip Blumstein and Pepper Schwartz report that in most of 3,600 married couples surveyed in the late 1970s, working wives were still expected to do the housework: "Working wives do less housework than homemakers, but they still do the vast bulk of what needs to be done" (1983, p. 144).

A Question of Fairness

If you are (or will be) a wife contributing to the provider role in the marriage, you may balk at also being expected to meet traditional female cooking and housekeeping roles. You may be more likely to perceive your marriage roles as unfair and unfavorable to yourself. The question of equity in marital roles across the life cycle was examined by two Iowa State University sociologists—Robert B. Schafer and Patricia M. Keith. They questioned over 300 couples living in Iowa in 1980 about the fairness of the breadwinner role, child care, cooking and housekeeping duties (among other family roles).

They found that married women with at least one child under six in the family expressed the greatest dissatisfaction. Among these women, almost one-third thought that their cooking and housekeeping duties were unfair and unfavorable to them. In contrast, less than one-fourteenth of married men with such a young child in their households felt that the cooking and housekeeping duties were unfair to them. Almost half of the men admitted that such duties were not equal and that they benefited from the inequity.

Some wives also thought that child-care responsibilities were unfair. Of the wives with young children, one-fifth felt that the parenthood role was unfair to them, compared with two-fifths of fathers with young children who admitted an inequity existed that favored them.

Sociologist Jessie Bernard argues that men benefit more from marriage than do women. Many men see marriage as a means for providing themselves with a wife who will take care of their cooking and housekeeping needs, their young children, and now also contribute to the family's income. Women who feel such expectations are unfair, and who experience them in their marriages, may be more likely to divorce—assuming they can financially provide for themselves. And they also may be less interested in remarrying.

A larger number of divorced people in the nation brings with it an increase in the number of children whose parents have divorced. Many people marry to have their own children and, having achieved that goal, divorce and do not remarry. Some wait until their youngest child becomes a teenager before divorcing, while others take on child-care responsibilities as a single parent. Children demand considerable time and financial support. The next chapter takes up the matter of parenthood—in or out of marriage.

6/

Childfree or Parent?

Unlike some reversible life choices, parenthood is permanent. If you marry, for example, you can become unmarried. But once a parent always a parent. To become a parent—or not to—is one of the most important life choices you and your agemates will make, both for yourselves and the nation. The total number of children your cohort has will affect United States population growth rates and eventual population size, and thus will influence the future quality of life of your generation.

Before making the choice, you may ask: "Why have children?" or "How many children shall I have?" I believe an equally important question to consider is: "Why live with children?" Pragmatically speaking, parenthood is much more a matter of rearing children than giving birth to them. For some people, the period of rearing children is a most important time. They feel that the heart of family life is living with children, caring for them, and trying to shape their values and beliefs. According to the National Center for Opinion Research, in 1982 many more adults expressed "a very great deal of satisfaction" from their family lives than from their health, friendships, hobbies, or the place where they lived.

Becoming a parent is more a matter of choice than it once was. Most children born in the United States today are wanted children. Among the mothers in their midteens through their midforties who were surveyed by the National Survey of Family Growth in 1976, only one-tenth of whites and one-quarter of blacks reported having had a child that at conception was "not wanted" or "probably not wanted."

One reason for the high proportions of wanted children is that by the mid-1970s most married women in their fertile years were using contraceptive methods—seventy percent of whites and sixty percent of blacks. By 1982 the figure was even higher—nine-tenths of sexually active women from fifteen through forty-four years old were using some method of contraception (including sterilization). Birth control is no longer a controversial issue for most people. Nine-tenths of adults interviewed in 1982 by the National Opinion Research Center said that birth control information should be available to anyone who wants it.

Another reason for the high proportions of wanted children is that abortion has become widely used, especially among unmarried women. According to national surveys taken since the late 1970s, two-fifths of women in the United States (and half of unmarried women), said they would consider having an abortion if they had an unwanted pregnancy. In the United States in 1980 there were three legal abortions for every seven births.

Given greater potential control over the biology of reproduction, parenthood now—more than ever before—depends on personal concerns and social values. One result is the short period in life during which most women give birth. Most women in the United States have finished giving birth by their late twenties or early thirties. Mothers thirty-five years old or over accounted for less than one-twentieth of all births in the United States in 1979. The period in life spent rearing children, on the other hand, continues until the last-born (or last-adopted) child has become independent—perhaps for decades.

Family sociologist Joan Aldous suggests thinking about family life as a career in which giving birth and rearing children can be of great importance. Whatever you choose to do, the fact remains that having and raising children make significant demands on your time, energy, and resources. To assist you in making your own long-term choices about parenthood (or in better understanding those choices you have made by now), this chapter will present information about several facets of family life including:

1. Others' expectations of childlessness and family size.
2. The most common age for giving birth.
3. The consequences of parenthood choices for future population size.
4. Parenting values versus childfree values.
5. The kinds of households—family or nonfamily—projected for your cohort in 1995.

PARENTHOOD EXPECTATIONS

Knowing how many children other people expect to have may help you decide how many—if any—you want. Each year the Bureau of the Census asks several thousand women in the peak ages for giving birth (eighteen through thirty-four) how many children they have had so far, and how many more they expect to have in their lifetime. The questions are asked only of women because fertility statistics are based on information about mothers instead of fathers. The survey results are then used to estimate national fertility expectations.

The government survey does not ask women how many children they consider as "ideal." Ideal family size preferences often assume ideal conditions. The number of children a woman actually expects to have, on the other hand, usually is based on her current situation.

Just as there is a difference between ideal family size attitudes and the number of children a woman expects to have, there also is a difference between anticipated and actual fertility. Some women have more children than they intend, others have fewer. If a woman's circumstances change, then her fertility expectations also may change. That is probably why fertility surveys made in the late 1960s did not predict the drop in births that occurred after 1970. As birth expectations changed suddenly in the early 1970s, so did the number of children actually born.

Birth expectations have been low since the mid-1970s, after the larger families of the 1950s and 1960s suddenly went out of fashion. The proportion of young married women intending to have three or more children declined from over half in the late 1960s to one-quarter by the mid-1970s. Both whites and blacks intended to have fewer children. Among white wives in their late teens and early twenties, the average number of children they expected to have fell from three to two between 1967 and 1975. Over the same period, the lifetime births expected by black wives in the same age group declined from three to two-and-one-half.

By 1982, there were only small differences in fertility expectations among whites, blacks, and Hispanics. At that time, the women who were in the peak ages for giving birth—eighteen through thirty-four—had themselves been born during the Baby Boom years of 1948 through 1964. Among these women, whites and blacks expected to have somewhat fewer children than Hispanics (the figures were 2.0, 2.1, and 2.3 children respectively). Because blacks and Hispanics are numerical minorities, the birth expectations of whites largely determine the figure for the nation as a whole—which was 2.0 expected lifetime births.

Childlessness

Only a small minority of young women expect never to become mothers, but their numbers are increasing. As family size intentions diminished, expectations of permanent childlessness slightly increased. The proportion of young wives who said they never expect to become mothers grew from one to five percent between 1967 and 1980. Given that positive reasons do exist for not becoming a parent, and that childlessness can be involuntary, the voluntary decision not to have children perhaps should be called remaining "childfree" instead of being "childless."

Sociologist Jean E. Veevers reports that voluntarily childfree couples today often find themselves having to resist social pressures to have children. Childlessness, both involuntary and by choice, still is much less common than it was at times in the past. One-fifth of married women born between 1901 and 1909, for example, never had any children of their own. One reason was that their peak years for giving birth coincided with the Great Depression of the late 1920s and 1930s. Because of the harsh economic realities they faced, many women were highly motivated to avoid giving birth by effectively using the limited birth control methods available to them at that time—including voluntary abstinence, less frequent intercourse, diaphragms, and spermicides, and having their partners use withdrawal or condoms. Although abortion was illegal, it was used by some women.

Which women are most likely to remain voluntarily childfree? Not surprisingly, many are women who have attractive alternatives to motherhood. If you are a woman who plans to seek paid employment, to complete five or more years of college, or who aspires to a higher status job, you will be joining the group of women most likely never to have any children of their own. Those were the conclusions of a national survey of women who were eighteen through thirty-four years old in 1982.

Here are the details. Twice the proportion of employed women, as opposed to women not in the labor force, intended to remain childfree (one-seventh compared with one-fifteenth). Among employed women, those with higher-status jobs generally were the most likely to expect to be childfree. For example, almost one-fifth of women employed as managers, administrators, or professionals expected never to have any children. Educational differences also were important. Almost one-fifth of women who had completed five years of college intended to remain childfree. The comparable figure for high-school graduates who did not go on to college was only one-tenth.

Some links among education, occupation, and intending to be childfree are straightforward. A young woman postpones her first birth until she completes her education. Then she decides to postpone motherhood a few years longer after beginning to work full time, especially if she is striving toward a career in a higher-status occupation. The more she succeeds in achieving educational and occupational goals, the greater the "opportunity cost" to her in having her first child. Thus the longer she postpones her first birth for educational or career goals, the more likely she is to remain permanently childfree.

Who Expects to Have Children?

If women with attractive employment options are most likely to be childfree, which women are most likely to have large families? The Bureau of the

Census categorizes lifetime birth expectations of women by several characteristics which at one time were related with fertility:

1. Age.
2. Race/ethnicity.
3. Marital status.
4. Years of school completed.
5. Labor force status.
6. Occupation of employed women.
7. Family income.
8. Residence in a poverty area.
9. National region of residence.
10. Metropolitan/nonmetropolitan residence.

Of this long list of factors, only a few produced meaningful differences in
fertility expectations in 1982, and the differences were not large. The largest
expected family size averaged 2.3 children, and was reported by women
farm workers, Hispanics, high-school dropouts, and those who were not in
the labor force. The smallest intended family averaged slightly less than two
children (1.7) among women employed as managers or administrators, or
those women who had completed five or more years of college. Once again,
higher educational levels and employment status were among the most
important factors associated with lower family size expectations. Although
small differences in fertility expectations persist today, among those who
intend to become mothers, the two-child family is becoming a widely held
expectation.

WHAT IS THE MOST COMMON AGE FOR GIVING BIRTH?

Age is, of course, an important trait determining which women are most
likely to give birth in any given year. If you are planning to postpone having
children until your late twenties, you may be pleasantly surprised to learn
that you have considerable company. More women recently have been having their children later in life. For decades the most common age for giving
birth was during the late teens and early twenties. But by 1982, the birth
rate of women in their late twenties was higher than that of younger women
(Table 6-1).

White mothers are more likely to give birth at a later age than either
black or Hispanic mothers. In the late 1970s, the fertility rates of white
women in their early twenties were about the same as those in their late
twenties. By the early 1980s, however, the most common age for giving
birth among whites had become the late twenties. In contrast, the peak years
for giving birth for Hispanics and blacks were still the early twenties, accord-

Table 6-1   What is the Peak Age for Giving Birth? For a First Birth?
Total Births and First Births Occurring in the 12 Months before June,
1982, in Selected Age Groups

Age of Women	Births Per 1,000 Women	First Births Per 1,000 Women
18 to 24 years	88.3	51.3
25 to 29 years	110.7	34.3
30 to 34 years	73.5	14.1
35 to 39 years	29.4	1.7
40 to 44 years	10.5	0.7
Average for 18 to 44 years	70.5	25.9

Source: Bureau of the Census, "Fertility of American Women: June 1982
(Advance Report)," *Current Population Reports,* Series P-20, No. 379 (May
1983).

ing to birth registration information collected from those twenty-two states
that identify Hispanic origin on their birth certificates.

As a result of more women postponing their first birth beyond their early
twenties, in 1982 first births accounted for slightly less than one-third of all
births to women in their late twenties, and one-fifth of all births to women
in their early thirties. Compared with younger mothers, those giving birth
after age thirty were more likely to be married, have had some college education, be employed, work in a professional occupation, and have a family
income of more than $25,000 in 1982. Once again, the importance of edu-
cation and occupation in parenthood decisions is seen. If women with better
educations, and working in higher-status jobs, have children at all, they are
more likely than other women to postpone having them until their late twenties or early thirties.

PARENTING CHOICES AND FUTURE POPULATION SIZE

Because sheer numbers of people are important to many of our life prospects, let us consider how individual parenthood choices can affect future
population size. The issue is both a matter of how many children you decide
to have (if any), and the consequences for you of the numbers of children
millions of other people have.

Few people take into account the nation's population size, decades in the
future, when deciding whether to have a child. But what difference would
one extra child per woman make to the future population? When you multiply that decision by the many millions of women coming into their most

fertile time of life during the next several decades, small differences in family size produce large differences in total population size.

Let us see how many more people there would be in the United States if we assumed different completed family sizes. The Bureau of the Census used three levels of fertility in its most recent population projections—1.6, 1.9, and 2.3 lifetime births per woman. Notice that the difference between the highest and the lowest official fertility assumptions is not even one child.

In 1984, 236 million people were living in the United States. How would that figure change under each official fertility assumption? For each fertility assumption, let us assume the same levels of future migration and mortality: (1) a net balance of 450,000 immigrants coming to the United States each year; and (2) a gradual improvement in life expectancy.

With only 1.6 births per woman, not enough children will be produced to replace the population. Because some people die as children and young adults before having their own children, an average of 2.1 children per couple is needed to replace the population over the long run. An average of 1.6 children will cause the population to begin to decline after reaching a maximum size of 276 million in 2020. If such a low level of fertility persisted, the 258 million people projected for 2050 would be only nine percent larger than the 1984 population size.

The middle, and most likely, fertility assumption of 1.9 children also is less than that needed to replace the population. If it were not for the assumption of almost one-half million immigrants coming to live in the United States each year, the population would begin to decline within the next century. But the growth provided by immigration is enough to offset such a potential decline. Under this set of assumptions, the population would reach 309 million by 2050. It would still be slowly growing, and would be thirty percent larger than the 1984 population.

Although the highest fertility assumption of 2.3 children is possible, it is not thought to be probable. For the nation to return to such an average family size, the following would have to occur:

1. A decline in female labor-force participation.
2. A younger age at first marriage for women.
3. An increase in the proportion of women who are married.
4. A decline in the educational attainment of women.

Because recent trends are toward greater labor-force participation of women, more postponed marriage, more unmarried people, and higher levels of education for women, demographers expect women to average two children or less each for the next several decades. However unlikely it may seem today, if women did have an average of 2.3 children in the future, a large and growing population would result. By 2050, there would be 380 million people living in the United States—sixty-one percent more than in 1984.

Under the lowest and the middle levels of fertility (1.6 and 1.9 children, respectively), the population not only would be growing slowly (or even declining) by the early twenty-first century, it also would be rapidly aging. Many people born in the late 1960s will live to see the 2040s and 2050s. If you will be one of these, you may experience the consequences of living in a much larger population if high fertility returns, or of living in a declining population with high proportions of elderly people if lower fertility conditions prevail.

We shall examine later (in Chapter Eight) the consequences for retired people of an older and declining population, as opposed to a younger and growing population. For our present purposes, the point is that current parenthood choices are shaping our future national population prospects—both the total number of people we shall be living with, and the relative burden of supporting the elderly population.

Race

Among women in their most fertile years in 1982, black women intended to have only somewhat more children (seven percent more) than did white women. The actual fertility rates of blacks in 1980, however, were much higher (thirty percent higher) than white rates, in part due to racial differences in the access to, and use of, birth control methods. Should a higher black than white fertility rate continue for decades, the proportion of the total population that is black would increase.

The Bureau of the Census assumes this will happen. Assuming an average of 1.9 children per woman generally, and a higher number for black women, the black portion of the total United States population would grow from one-eighth in 1984 to one-sixth in 2050. Similarly, if the higher levels of Hispanic fertility persist, the proportion of Hispanics would increase independently of the effects of immigration.

PARENTING VALUES AND CHILDFREE VALUES

Let us return to your own fertility decisions—past, present, or future. Just as sociologists believe that most people make their marriage choices according to their social values, they also believe that most people make their parenting choices to achieve certain social values. If you understand what people expect from having and raising children, then you can understand why they choose to become parents. From this perspective, variations in voluntary childlessness, family size, and births to unmarried women all can result from differing social values about children and family life.

What is the value of a child? The numerous reasons why people have children can be summarized into several general categories:

1. To have a child to love and nurture.
2. For adult status and social identity.
3. To expand oneself, "immortality."
4. To respond to social, religious, or moral expectations regarding altruism, sexuality, virtue.
5. To create kinship ties.
6. To bring more stimulation, novelty, and fun into one's life.
7. To exercise one's creativity and competence by accomplishing the expectations of being a parent.
8. To have power and influence over another person.
9. To respond to social competition or comparisons.
10. For the child's eventual economic utility to oneself.

In reading this list, you may have found some items that you agree are good general reasons for having a child (whether they apply to you personally or not), and others that you think are not. I have expressed several of these widely held values about children and family life in a questionnaire format (Questionnaire D) similar to the one used in the previous chapter. The first part of the questionnaire contains positive reasons for having a child, the second half consists of positive reasons for remaining childfree. Each of the twelve value positions should be self-explanatory.

Although any such questionnaire is oversimplified, the process of filling it out may help you think about your own values about having children of your own, and especially about living with children (whether your own or adopted). Most of the "parenting values" involve caring for, and spending time with, children. Most of the "childfree values" give higher priority to personal independence and being self-sufficient.

A high score in either parenting or childfree categories is less important than the difference between the two scores. A large difference indicates a strong preference for living with children or not. A small difference, say five points or less, shows that you probably are ambivalent about becoming a parent, or if you already are one, about having more children. Because of the permanence of parenthood, if you are ambivalent you may wish to postpone having a child (or having more children) until you strongly favor several parenting values over childfree values.

A FAMILY IN 1995?

When making choices about living with children, a good question to ask yourself is whether you want to be living in a family setting in, say, ten or

QUESTIONNAIRE D: **Personal Questionnaire about Ideal Standards for Parenting or Being Childfree**

Procedure: Place a checkmark to indicate whether, and how strongly, you desire or reject a given value. Add up your checkmarks in each column, and multiply them by one to five points depending on how strongly you feel about each. By adding these figures together, you obtain your total PARENTING SCORE or CHILDFREE SCORE.

	Strongly Disagree				Strongly Agree
	1	2	3	4	5
PARENTING VALUES					
1. Children are the heart of family life	___	___	___	___	___
2. Children bring out the best in you	___	___	___	___	___
3. Family life is more satisfying than friends, work, or hobbies	___	___	___	___	___
4. Teaching young children basic skills is enjoyable	___	___	___	___	___
5. I enjoy being needed by children	___	___	___	___	___
6. If need be, grown children should help their elderly parents	___	___	___	___	___
Total Checkmarks	___	___	___	___	___
Multiply by:	× 1	× 2	× 3	× 4	× 5
Subtotals	___	___	___	___	___

Total PARENTING SCORE = _____ (Add five subtotals together)

(Continued on following page.)

fifteen years. Most people do. That does not mean that you have to—you can choose not to.

For our present purposes, let us define a "family" both as the dictionary and the Bureau of the Census do: two or more people living together who are related by blood, marriage, or adoption. If you choose not to live in a family setting, you have only two alternatives—either living alone or with nonrelatives. Because families, by definition, can result from either marriage or parenting choices (both your own and those of your parents), we now shall combine the marriage patterns discussed in the previous chapter with the fertility choices covered in this one.

(Questionnaire D continued.)

	Strongly Disagree				Strongly Agree
	1	2	3	4	5

CHILDFREE VALUES

1. Adulthood can be satisfying without parenthood
2. I prefer to invest my resources in goals other than raising a child
3. Work, friends, or hobbies are more satisfying than family life
4. I want to know myself better before bringing a child into my life

5. I enjoy being independent
6. Elderly parents should not depend on their grown children

Total Checkmarks
Multiply by: × 1 × 2 × 3 × 4 × 5

Subtotals
Total CHILDFREE SCORE = _____ (Add five subtotals together)

From your: PARENTING SCORE _____
SUBTRACT your: CHILDFREE SCORE − _____
Difference (plus or minus) = _____

Whether living in a family or not, most people will be living in what the Census Bureau calls "private households": all persons occupying a housing unit (a house, apartment, group of rooms, or a single room). Households in which at least one family member owns or rents the housing unit are called "family households." All other households (people living alone or with non-relatives) are called "nonfamily households." The small minority of people not living in private households resides in institutional settings (a military barracks, a college dormitory, a hospital, a prison, etc.).

A word about a change in the definition of the term "householder": households are linked to birth cohorts through the age of the "house-holder"—the adult responsible for maintaining the household. Before 1980, the Census Bureau always classified the husband as the "head of household" in married-couple families. Current Census Bureau practice is to have the household members themselves name one person as the "householder."

That person usually is the one in whose name the home is owned or rented. If a home is jointly owned or rented by a married couple, either the husband or the wife could be named by family members as the "householder."

To help you think about your own family and household choices, I have illustrated the household types projected for 1995 by the age of the house-holder (Figure 6-1). I chose 1995 because people born in the late 1960s will be in their late twenties at that time and almost all will be living in private households. The "family households" have been further specified as those in which the owner or renter is married and living with his or her spouse (Married-Couple Households), and those in which the household head is not (Other Family Households).

In which of the three household types will you be living in 1995—non-family, other family, or married couple? Another way of asking the question is: "Will 1995 be the point in your life when you will be living alone, as a single parent living with your offspring, or as a married person living with your spouse?"

Most—nine-tenths—of "nonfamily households" today are people living alone. The main reason for living alone differs for the sexes. Widows made up over half of the women living by themselves in 1981, for example, while almost two-thirds of men living alone had never married.

Less than half of the "other family households" in 1981 were siblings, aunts, uncles, grandchildren, or other nonparent-child relatives living together. Over half of the "other family households" in 1981 were single-parent families—nine-tenths of which were headed by women. While many children in single-parent families are living with divorced or widowed mothers, the number living with never-married mothers has been increasing. Of all babies born between 1950 and 1979, for example, the proportion born to unmarried mothers increased for whites from one-fiftieth to one-tenth, and for nonwhites from one-sixth to one-half. The difficulties faced by women rearing children alone is reflected in the title chosen by Sheila B. Kamerman for her book about working mothers: *Parenting in an Unresponsive Society—Managing Work and Family.*

If you were born at any time between 1921 and 1981, Figure 6-1 shows you your cohort's distribution of family types projected for 1995. To help you think about your options, we can examine in some detail projections for three different cohorts—people born in the 1960s, the 1950s, and the 1920s. If you are a member of another cohort, Figure 6-1 shows you which cohort discussed in detail is most like your own.

For each selected cohort, I will briefly present both the percentages and the odds of a person being in one or another category. If you happen to be a member of one of these cohorts, the percentages and approximate odds should be helpful in showing you what to expect. Even though you may beat the odds, chances are they will apply to many people you know. The information about cohorts other than your own can give you some insight into the

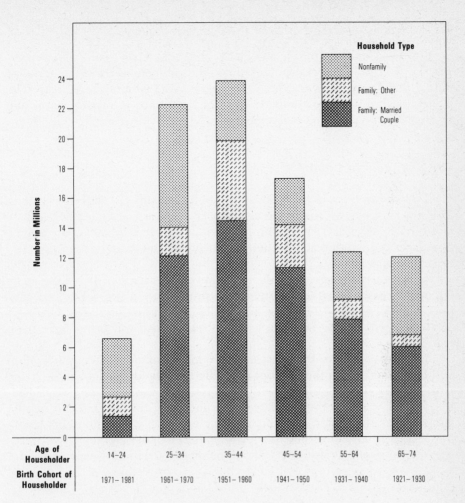

Figure 6-1. How Numerous Will Family Households Be? Households by Type and Age of Householder, United States, 1995.

Source: Bureau of the Census, "Projections of the Number of Households and Families: 1979 to 1995," *Current Population Reports,* Series P-25, No. 805 (May 1979).

living arrangements expected for friends and relatives who are older or younger than you.

For the sake of simplicity and clarity, I use the term "will" when referring to the 1995 projections. Of course, the projections "will" materialize only if the assumptions on which they were based turn out to be true. The projections are extrapolations to 1995 of the trends in marital status and household type recorded between 1964 and 1978.

1961-1970 Birth Cohort

If you were born in the 1960s, by 1995 the odds are slightly less than fifty-fifty that you will be living as a spouse in a husband/wife family. Back in 1980, living as a married couple was much more popular—then almost two-thirds of householders in their late twenties and early thirties were living with a spouse.

Postponed marriage, and deciding never to marry, will be the most important reasons for the decline in the proportion of young married couples. Most of the householders in their late twenties and early thirties in 1995 who will not be living in a family setting also will never have been married.

A second reason for the decreasing proportion of married-couple families will be an increase in the number of family householders who will be living with children—but not living with a spouse. Nine-tenths of the "other family" householders in their late twenties and early thirties in 1995 will be women. If these women are similar to single-parent women householders in 1981, then almost all will be living with children under eighteen, two-thirds will be white, and almost one-half will be divorced and not remarried.

If you were born between 1961 and 1970, you can expect the following odds of living in a married-couple, other family, or a nonfamily household:

1961-70 Cohort (Age 25-34 in 1995)

	Percent	Odds
Husband-Wife Family Households	45	3 in 7
Other Family Households	18	1 in 6
Nonfamily Households	37	3 in 8
Total Percentage	100%	

1951-1960 Birth Cohort

The odds of living in a married-couple household are better among people in the next older cohort. If you will be in your late thirties or early forties in 1995, chances are not quite two in three that you will be living in a husband-wife household. One reason is that few people will be postponing marriage by this age. Another reason is that many who had divorced will have remarried. The popularity of living as a married couple in 1995, nevertheless, will be less than it was in 1980. Married couples as a proportion of all householders in this age group are projected to decline from seven-tenths in 1980 to six-tenths in 1995.

The late thirties and early forties are the peak years for single parenthood. People that age have lived long enough to have married, have had children, and have divorced. But their children are still young enough to be living at home with a parent. Single-parent families are expected to increase—both in proportion and in total number. High divorce rates, low remarriage rates, and growing numbers of births to unmarried mothers all will contribute to the trend. The proportion of "other family" householders among all householders aged thirty-five through forty-four will increase from seventeen percent in 1980 to twenty-two percent in 1995. For women born in the 1950s, the odds of being a single parent by 1995 are better than one in five.

A large change in cohort sizes will make single-parent families much more visible in the mid-1990s than they were in 1980. The small cohort born at the end of the Great Depression and during World War II (1936 through 1945) was in its late thirties and early forties in 1980. By 1995 people that age will have been born between 1951 and 1960—a major part of the Baby Boom cohort. The replacement of a small cohort with a large cohort combined with a greater incidence of single parenthood will more than double the number of "other family" households by 1995.

1951-60 Cohort (Age 35-44 in 1995)

	Percent	Odds
Husband-Wife Family Households	61	3 in 5
Other Family Households	22	2 in 9
Nonfamily Households	17	1 in 6
Total Percentage	100%	

1921-1930 Cohort

From age forty on, the proportion of single-parent households gradually declines. Few births occur, and children grow up and leave home. Most householders from their early forties through their early sixties currently are married and living with their spouses—and two-thirds are expected to be in 1995. But as male mortality rises rapidly from the late fifties onward, widowhood results in increasing numbers of women living alone in "nonfamily households."

If you will be in your late sixties or early seventies in 1995, you can expect that half of all households will be married couples. Almost as many households will be "nonfamily." Over three-fourths of the nonfamily house-holders will be women. And if these women are similar to those of the cor-responding age and household type in 1981, then four-fifths will be wid-owed, and almost all (ninety-eight percent) will be living alone.

1921-30 Cohort (Age 65-74 in 1995)

	Percent	Odds
Husband-Wife Family Households	49	1 in 2
Other Family Households	7	1 in 15
Nonfamily Households	44	2 in 5
Total Pecentage	100%	

Your family choices in your twenties and thirties will (or already have) set certain constraints on your options in your forties and fifties. If you choose to be unmarried or never to have children, for example, you will have fewer kinship ties in middle age. If you are not living in a husband-wife household, as another example, you will be less likely to own your own home or to be a long-term resident of a community. The following chapter takes up these, and some other matters, that revolve around decisions to rent or own your home, and to move to a new residence or to stay where you are.

7/

Homeowner or Renter?
Mover or Stayer?

Many people in their early twenties are in transition, their lives in a state of constant change. Few remain at the same address more than two or three years. Most rent instead of owning their homes. Most are either still in school or working at entry-level jobs. Most have never married, and either live alone or share their housing with nonrelatives. And of those who have married, few have school-age children.

Twenty years later, several things haved changed considerably. Because many people in their early forties have voluntarily chosen to narrow their options, their lives have become more predictable both to themselves and others. At this stage in life, most people are married (or remarried) and living with their spouses. The majority are homeowners who stay at the same address for several years at a time. Almost all are employed (or are married to someone who is). Most have had children, and many still have children living at home. By their early forties, many people have developed ties to a locality through their work and other interests, and through the activities of their spouses and/or children.

Change still occurs, of course. Choices persist and are influenced by the size of a person's birth cohort. But the arenas of action are different than they were twenty years earlier. Middle-aged people have tried to create a certain way of life for themselves, and are midway in the process of living that life. Not everyone achieves their midlife goals, but everyone experiences the consequences of actions taken when they were younger. As described in previous chapters, midlife circumstances are affected by decisions made in a person's teens, twenties, and thirties about education, employment, marriage, and having children.

If you are in your teens or early twenties, what do you gain by learning more about how middle-aged people live? For one thing, you can see just how choices made as young adults influenced the lives of some of the older people you know. You also can look at the choices you are making now, or in the next few years, and ask yourself what their consequences may be for you in twenty or thirty years. By understanding the process better, you may improve your chances of achieving the life you want when you become middle-aged.

To help you gain some of these insights, I have chosen two topics that show some consequences of choices made earlier in life, are intrinsically important aspects of life, are readily described with available population data, and are involved in the process of developing community ties by middle age—becoming a homeowner, and staying in one location. Other significant on-going processes in middle age (that are beyond the scope of our present purposes), include nurturing family life, pursuing or changing a career, gaining civic influence, or establishing financial resources. Specifically, this chapter addresses the following issues and questions:

1. Housing choices, community ties, and moving.
2. How strongly you feel about renting or homeowning.
3. Who owns their own homes? Who rents?
4. How will population change influence first-home buying prospects in the 1980s and 1990s?
5. Who is most—and least—likely to change residences?

HOUSING CHOICES, COMMUNITY TIES, AND MOVING

The place where you live refers to both the dwelling itself and the community within which your home is located. Because you spend several hours each day (and night) within your home, it probably is a major element in how you perceive the quality of your life. The physical structure and amenities of a residence, for example, can influence your family life. Overcrowded housing can create stress among family members, just as a home that provides adequate space and privacy can improve household relations. The quality of housing is so important to some people that they spend a large portion of their earnings on housing expenses. One-third of the monthly incomes of recent home buyers in 1982, for example, went just for their home mortgage payments.

Many people consider their housing and its location a major means of expressing their particular values about life, including their preferences for: (1) urban, suburban, or rural life styles; (2) living in a particular neighborhood, city, state, or region of the United States; (3) possibly benefiting their children by residing in a certain elementary and secondary school district; or (4) living close to people of similar racial, religious, ethnic, or economic backgrounds. You may or may not share these values. But many people who do feel this way also assume that homes reflect a person's general status in society—that homes are unusually visible status symbols.

The importance of housing and locality for many people in the United States seemingly contradicts another major characteristic of life in that society—the rapid rate with which many change residences. Over one-fifth of all householders changed addresses during the year preceding the 1980 census. Actually there is no contradiction. Most people in the United States are willing to move in order to find the housing and location that best satisfies their major goals in life, including forming their own families and becoming homeowners. As we shall see later in this chapter, moving rapidly diminishes in frequency after people reach their forties and develop ties to a job, a home, and a community.

In spite of the importance of housing for our social lives, with a few major exceptions the subject has received relatively little attention by sociologists. Housing sociologists Kenneth R. Tremblay, Jr., and Don A. Dillman have categorized the sparse sociological research on housing into three perspectives. First are researchers interested in the consequences that housing has for individuals and the society as a whole, especially as it impinges on family life. Second are those who see housing as a social problem, and whose research is directed at formulating social policies aimed at reducing social conflict generated by housing inequities. Third are sociologists concerned about how housing affects the everyday interactions among people.

The material presented in this chapter follows the first perspective. I assume that people have certain criteria (values) about the housing and locality they prefer, and that they evaluate their current residence against their criteria. If their housing or locality does not satisfy them, they consider either moving, altering their present home, or changing their expectations. The more strongly they feel about their housing values, I assume the more willing they are to give housing priority over other major life goals. Thus values about housing are, from this perspective, the starting point of the discussion.

What are your values about the residence and the locality in which you would like to live? A useful way to organize your thoughts about the matter is to consider whether you would prefer being a homeowner or a renter.

HOMEOWNER OR RENTER?

Homeownership is a goal for many people—and one that most eventually achieve. Two-thirds of all housing units in the United States in 1980 were occupied by homeowners. The Census Bureau defines homeowners as people holding title to the place in which they live even if it is mortgaged or otherwise not fully paid for. People living in housing owned by someone else are defined by the Census Bureau as renting, whether or not they pay a cash rent. The terms homeowner and householder are easily confused. House-holder simply means a person who occupies some housing as his or her home. All homeowners are householders. But not all householders are home-owners—some are renters.

Renting and Homeowning Values

Which do you prefer? Renting or owning? Some people would like to have more than one home if money were no object—an apartment down-town perhaps, and a house in the suburbs, plus a summer house at the beach or in the mountains. But realistically most of us live in only one place, our "primary residence." We cannot afford to fulfill all our housing desires by owning or renting several homes simultaneously, so we must set our priori-ties about what we want most from the one place where we will be living.

The personal questionnaire format we used in previous chapters is also helpful for sorting out values about housing. Five widely held reasons for renting, and five for homeowning, are listed in Questionnaire E. The ques-tionnaire will serve you better if you make a copy of it and fill it out twice. The first time, think about the one place where you would like to live now—considering your present educational, employment, marriage, and family statuses. The second time, fill it out in terms of the life situation you hope to have twenty or thirty years from now. Such a brief questionnaire is not, of course, a scientific survey about housing values. But it may indicate some of your preferences about where you want to live, both now and in the future.

For our present purposes what counts is how strongly you feel about either housing alternative. A difference between your homeowner and renter scores of ten points or more reflects a consistent and strong prefer-ence. You know what you want and why you want it. You may be willing to make sacrifices, or to put up with several inconveniences, to live the way you prefer. A narrower gap between the two scores shows a less consistent preference. You may wish to move from tenant to homeowner status, for example, but you may be less willing than a person with stronger desires for homeownership to forego other things in order to save for a downpayment.

Ambivalence about owning or renting is indicated by a difference in scores of five points or less. You may want the best of both worlds. Or you may have no strong feelings either way. High scores on both options mean you want to combine the advantages of renting and of owning. You may have in mind renting a suburban house, for example, or owning a high-rise, down-town condominium. At the other extreme, low scores on both options mean that your housing preferences are not that important to you. Everyone must live somewhere. But you may be willing to let other people's housing pref-erences (your spouse's, for example) determine where you will live.

You may eventually intend to own your own home—most people do. But actually becoming a homeowner, of course, depends on more than just your own personal values. It also hinges on where you live, your age, your marital status, and, to a smaller degree, your family income. You can better judge how realistic your own housing goals are by reviewing facts about those who already are renting or owning.

City and State Differences in Renting or Owning

You can increase your chances of becoming a homeowner by moving away from a large city. Although suburban living is highly related with homeownership, homeowning is even slightly more common beyond the suburbs. Land and housing generally cost less away from urban areas. Three-quarters of householders living in nonmetropolitan areas in the United States own their own homes. In contrast, on the average, only half are homeowners in the larger cities in the United States.

The most extreme cases of cities in which renting is a way of life are listed in the top half of Table 7-1. Renting in these large cities is a permanent aspect of life for most people, and not a transition to eventual homeownership. The homeownership rate in each of these cities is far below that of the state in which the city is located. As examples, the homeownership rate for New Jersey in 1980 was almost triple that for Newark, and the rate for New York state was more than double the figure for New York City. Assuming they have the opportunity, people living in these eight cities would greatly improve their chances for homeownership by moving to the suburbs or beyond.

City life does not necessarily mean renting. In almost all cities in the United States, between two-fifths and three-fifths of householders own their own homes. The rates of homeownership in some smaller cities approach the levels of the states in which they are located. If you want to combine urban living with homeownership, you may wish to consider moving to a smaller city like one of those listed in the bottom half of Table 7-1. San Jose, California, for example, has a higher homeownership rate than that of the state of California. (If the city you are interested in is not in Table 7-1, it may be among the fifty-eight cities listed in the source cited for that table.)

What accounts for the differences in homeownership rates among cities, and among states? In some states, an unusually high cost of homes reduces the proportions of people who can afford to be homeowners. The most expensive state for owning your own home, for example, is Hawaii. In 1980, the median value of a one-family house in that state was $118,100—two-and-one-half times the national average of $47,200. As may be expected, fewer householders owned their homes in Hawaii than in any other state except New York. The problem in New York state was not the high cost of homes: the average one-family house was worth $45,600—slightly less than

QUESTIONNAIRE E: **Personal Questionnaire about Renting and Homeowning Values**

Procedure: Place a checkmark to indicate how strongly you desire or reject a given value. Add up your checkmarks in each column, and multiply them by one to five points depending on how strongly you feel about each. By adding these figures together, you obtain your total HOMEOWNER or RENTER scores.

	Strongly Reject				Strongly Desire
	1	2	3	4	5

RENTING VALUES:

1. Low financial commitment — no large downpayment required
2. Less monthly expense — lower cost of renting than buying
3. Less commuting — living closer to work
4. Greater geographic mobility — twelve-month lease
5. Freedom from responsibility for care of housing unit and grounds

	1	2	3	4	5
Total Checkmarks	____	____	____	____	____
Multiply by:	× 1	× 2	× 3	× 4	× 5
Subtotals	____	____	____	____	____

Total RENTER SCORE = _____ (Add five subtotals together.)

(Questionnaire E continued on following page.)

the national average. The homeownership rate in New York state was the lowest in the nation largely because over two-fifths of all year-round housing units in the state are located in New York City—where renting is the norm.

Aside from such local factors as housing costs, or living in an large city, what else explains why some people rent while others are homeowners? As we shall see, a large part of the story involves certain choices made earlier in life.

Who Rents?

If you choose to live alone after being divorced, widowed, or never having been married in the first place, then one consequence is that you are

(Questionnaire E Continued.)

	Strongly Reject				Strongly Desire
	1	2	3	4	5

HOMEOWNING VALUES:

1. Pride of ownership — having a place to call your own ____ ____ ____ ____ ____
2. Building financial equity in a home ____ ____ ____ ____ ____
3. Greater privacy — having a single family, detached dwelling ____ ____ ____ ____ ____
4. Your own personal outside space — having a yard or garden ____ ____ ____ ____ ____
5. Freedom to alter your home as you see fit ____ ____ ____ ____ ____

Total Checkmarks ____ ____ ____ ____ ____
Multiply by: × 1 × 2 × 3 × 4 × 5

Subtotals ____ ____ ____ ____ ____
Total HOMEOWNER SCORE = ____ (Add five subtotals together.)

From your: HOMEOWNER SCORE ____
Subtract your: RENTER SCORE − ____
Difference (plus or minus) = ____

highly likely to be a renter. Although the number of unmarried homeowners is growing, the great majority still rent—in 1980, four-fifths of all people living alone, and who were between the ages of fifteen and forty-four, were tenants. If you live alone and have only your own income available to pay for housing (in contrast to two-earner married couples), you may prefer the lower monthly cost and no large downpayment of renting. The freedom from maintenance responsibilities that renting offers also may attract you, since you would not have anyone else living in your household to help you maintain your own house and yard.

If you decide to live with someone else while unmarried, you reduce the likelihood of being a renter—but not by much. In 1980, over two-thirds of unmarried family heads in their early forties and younger were tenants. They were primarily never-married or divorced single parents living with their children. They may have wanted more living space for their families, but could not afford to buy their own homes. With only one adult earner in the

Table 7-1   In Which Cities Was Renting—or Homeownership—a Way of Life in 1980?

	Homeownership Rate*	
City, State	City	State
LOW HOMEOWNERSHIP CITIES:		
1. Newark, New Jersey	21%	62%
2. New York, New York	23%	49%
3. Boston, Massachusetts	27%	58%
4. San Francisco, California	34%	56%
5. Miami, Florida	34%	68%
6. Washington, D.C.	36%	—
7. Cincinnati, Ohio	38%	68%
8. Chicago, Illinois	39%	63%
HIGH HOMEOWNERSHIP CITIES:		
1. Phoenix, Arizona	65%	68%
2. Virginia Beach, Virginia	64%	66%
3. Toledo, Ohio	63%	68%
4. Oklahoma City, Oklahoma . .	63%	71%
5. Jacksonville, Florida	63%	68%
6. San Jose, California	62%	56%
7. Omaha, Nebraska	61%	68%
8. Tulsa, Oklahoma	61%	71%

*Owner-occupied dwellings as a percentage of all year-round, occupied housing units.

Source: U.S. Bureau of the Census, *Statistical Abstract of the United States:* 1984 (104th Ed.), Tables 1340, 1341, pp. 749–751.

family, there was not enough money in the household budget to make a downpayment on a house, or to undertake large monthly mortgage payments.

What if you decide to marry? Then you greatly increase your chances of becoming a homeowner—but not at first. Although most married couples eventually become homeowners, young, newly married couples are more likely to be tenants. If you are married, in your early twenties and renting, you have a lot of company. In 1980, almost two-thirds of married householders under twenty-five were renters. Regardless of their homeowning desires, at that stage in life few are able to make a downpayment on a house.

Saving for a downpayment on a house while renting is a major endeavor of many married couples in their early and mid-twenties. Most first-home

buyers make their downpayments entirely from their own savings and investments—over two-thirds did so in 1982. And the amount of money involved
is large. In that same year the average downpayment paid by first-time home
buyers was $8,900—fifteen percent of the average first-home price of
$58,900.

If your parents or other relatives help you with the downpayment, consider yourself fortunate. Most people are not so lucky. Only one-tenth of
first-home buyers received such assistance in 1982. Surprising as it may
seem, sociologist John C. Henretta has documented that parents' incomes
alone had no effect on the probability of their grown children becoming
homeowners. Even if your parents can afford to help, they may not.

Who Owns Their Own Homes?

It takes years for most couples to save for a downpayment on a home.
When husbands and wives both work and are childless, they enjoy two
advantages for saving. Their family incomes generally are much higher than
married couples with only one adult earner. And without any child-care
expenses, they can save more of their income for a downpayment on a home.
In recent years, childless first-home buyers have become the norm. Among
first-home buyers in 1980, married couples without children outnumbered
those with children by four to three. What this means is that the earlier in
life you begin having children, the longer you are likely to remain a tenant—
other things being equal.

The financial realities of becoming a homeowner usually result in first-
home buyers being in their late twenties or early thirties—in 1980 only fifteen percent were less than twenty-five years old. If you are almost thirty
when you buy your first home, you would not be behind the average. In fact,
you would be typical—the average age of first-home buyers in 1982 was
twenty-nine.

Although two-thirds of all householders own their own homes, the homeownership figure is even higher for those with certain characteristics. Ninety
percent of families and individuals with incomes of $35,000 or over in 1979,
for example, owned their own homes in 1980. This shows how strong the
connection is between high income and homeownership.

But ability to pay is not the whole story. At one extreme, some wealthy
people prefer renting. Among householders with incomes of $100,000 or
more in 1979, one in eleven rented. At the other extreme, you do not need
to be wealthy to be a homeowner in the United States—houses come in all
price ranges. Our concern here is with homeownership itself, and not with
the separate matter of the monetary value of homes. The more willing you
are to live in an older, smaller, less conveniently located home, the greater
your chances of becoming a homeowner. Among families that earned less
than $10,000 in 1979, for example, almost half owned their own homes.

The Importance of Age and Marital Status for Homeownership

There is an unusually strong connection between being married, middle-aged, and a homeowner. Homeowners accounted for almost nine-tenths of all married couples in their late thirties or older in 1980. Only extremely strong social values about homeownership produce such consistent behavior among so many millions of people. Such potent social norms are reflected in public policies that encourage and subsidize homeownership. For example, widespread political support exists for tax laws that make interest payments on home mortgages—but not rents—tax deductible. Given strength of prevailing norms about homeownership, if you intend to be married in middle age, then chances are that you also expect to own your own home at that time.

On the average, homeownership is much more common among whites than among either blacks or Hispanics. In 1980, over two-thirds of white householders were homeowners, compared with less than half of black or Hispanic householders. The exact percentages were sixty-nine, forty-four, and forty-two percent respectively. Why is this? Does it mean that married blacks and Hispanics cannot expect to be homeowners when they become middle-aged? To what degree does discrimination reduce the homeowning opportunities of minority-group members?

In one attempt to answer the question for blacks, social demographers Suzanne M. Bianchi, Reynolds Farley, and Daphne Spain analyzed information from a large, national survey of housing taken by the government in 1977. The researchers knew that proportionately fewer blacks were married, middle-aged, had higher incomes, or were living outside large cities—all factors that, aside from direct racial discrimination in housing, would help explain the lower black homeownership rate.

Using appropriate methods, they held constant the effects on homeownership of black and white differences in age, income, education, family type, tenure, region, and metropolitan location. They concluded that if there had been no difference between blacks and whites on that list of factors, then hypothetically homeowners would have accounted for sixty-nine percent of all white householders, and sixty percent of all black householders. According to their study, blacks were almost as likely to be homeowners as whites with similar characteristics, but not quite. The difference in homeownership that remained—nine percentage points—was due to all other factors including possibly different values about homeownership, and racial discrimination in housing.

Another way to answer the question that includes Hispanics as well as blacks is to hold constant the effects on homeownership of just two factors—age and marital status. Since we know that homeownership is most characteristic of middle-aged married couples, let us examine homeownership rates by age within just that one marital status. Table 7-2 presents the results of such a comparison using information from the 1980 Census.

Table 7-2 When Does the Transition to Homeownership Occur?

Homeowners as a Percentage of All Married Householders Living with Their Spouses by Their Age, Race or Ethnicity, United States, 1980

	Percentage Home Owners		
Age of Married Householder	*White*	*Black*	*Hispanic* *
LOW HOMEOWNERSHIP AGES:			
15–24	38%	19%	18%
TRANSITIONAL AGES:			
25–29	61%	34%	36%
30–34	78%	51%	52%
HIGH HOMEOWNERSHIP AGES:			
35–44	86%	70%	65%
45–64	89%	76%	72%
65 and over	86%	72%	63%

*Hispanic people may be of any race.

Source: United States Bureau of the Census, *1980 Census of Housing,* "Components of Inventory Change: United States and Regions," HC80-4-1 (August 1983), Tables A7, A13, A19, pp. 68, 125, 182.

Notice the similar influence of age on homeownership. In all three groups homeownership was most characteristic of middle-aged people. Among married householders between forty-five and sixty-four years old in 1980, for example, homeowners accounted for three-quarters of blacks and Hispanics, and nine-tenths of whites. The major difference was in how early in life that homeownership was achieved. Whites became homeowners at younger ages than did either blacks or Hispanics. Among married couples in their twenties, for example, whites were almost twice as likely as either blacks or Hispanics to be homeowners. The transitional age where over half of householders were homeowners was the late twenties for whites, and the early thirties for the other two groups.

Let us take the analysis one step farther. Proportionately more blacks and Hispanics than whites live in large cities, and we know that fewer large-city residents own homes regardless of race or ethnic origin. So let us see what the situation is among people living outside large cities.

When all three factors favor homeownership—being married, middle-aged, and living outside large cities—black and Hispanic homeownership rates more closely approach those of whites. In 1980, four-fifths of such black and Hispanic householders owned their own homes compared with nine-tenths of such whites. A gap among whites, blacks, and Hispanics remained. But whether black, white, or Hispanic, for most middle-aged married couples in 1980, especially for those living outside large cities, homeownership had been an achievable goal.

POPULATION CHANGE AND HOMEOWNERSHIP PROSPECTS IN THE 1990s

Regardless of race or ethnic origin, everyone's homeowning prospects are closely linked with the size of their birth cohort. Smaller cohorts coming along each year reduce competition for first homes. With less competition, real home prices can decline (holding inflation constant). For example, the ease with which the Depression Babies bought their first homes in the 1960s was described in Chapter Two. Larger cohorts can place greater competition on the first-home housing market and increase prices. The early Baby Boom Babies, for example, paid more for their first homes in the mid- and late 1970s than had the Depression Babies who bought their first homes during the 1960s (after holding constant the effects of inflation).

What about the 1980s and the 1990s? How will population change influence the homeowning prospects then of people born from the late 1950s through the early 1970s—the last members of the Baby Boom and the early members of the Baby Bust cohorts?

As a first step in answering that question, let us assume that the average age of first-home buyers will be twenty-eight through the end of this century. This would be in line with recent facts—between 1976 and 1981 the average age of first-time home buyers was twenty-eight, and in 1982 it was twenty-nine. By so doing, we can roughly estimate when younger cohorts will be coming into the peak ages for buying their first home. For example, the average person born in 1968 will be buying his or her first home in 1996 (1968 plus 28 equals 1996). This is not a forecast, of course, but merely a projection that assumes a certain average age of first-home buyers.

Next we need to know how much larger or smaller a cohort is than adjoining cohorts. If you were born between 1950 and 1973, Table 7-3 will show you how your cohort compared in size with others in 1983. Given our assumption about the average age of first-home buyers, we end up projecting in a general way how population change will influence first-home buying prospects between 1978 and 2001. This projection, of course, does not take into account possible small cohort differences in mortality or migration between 1983 and 2001—complexities that can be safely ignored for our present purposes.

Based on sheer numbers of people turning twenty-eight each year, population pressures on the first-home market will continue to increase and reach a peak in the late 1980s. People born around 1960 will be facing a

Table 7-3   How Will Cohort Size Influence First-Home Buying Prospects in the 1980s and 1990s?

Birth Years	Cohort Size in 1983	First Home Bought*
INCREASING POPULATION PRESSURE ON THE FIRST-HOME MARKET:		
1950–1952	11,521,000	1978–1980
1953–1955	12,289,000	1981–1983
1956–1958	12,932,000	1984–1986
PEAK POPULATION PRESSURE ON THE FIRST-HOME MARKET:		
1959–1961	13,378,000	1987–1989
DECREASING POPULATION PRESSURE ON THE FIRST-HOME MARKET:		
1962–1964	12,747,000	1990–1992
1965–1967	11,448,000	1993–1995
1968–1970	10,951,000	1996–1998
1971–1973	10,391,000	1999–2001

*Assuming the average age of first-time home buyers is twenty-eight.

Source: For cohort sizes in 1983 — U.S. Bureau of the Census, "Estimates of the Population of the United States, by Age, Sex, and Race: 1980 to 1983," *Current Population Reports,* Series P-25, No. 949 (May 1984), Table 1, p. 7.

more competitive first-home housing market than did people born five years before. Then, from 1990 on, the cohorts reaching their late twenties will rapidly diminish in size. In the late 1990s, there will be twenty-two percent fewer people turning twenty-eight each year than there were in the late 1980s. Fewer potential first-home buyers each year reduce demographic pressures on housing. The competition for first homes in 2000 will be lower than at any time during the previous twenty years.

Demand for housing is also closely linked with the formation of new households, and with general economic conditions. People often postpone marriage or giving birth when economic conditions are poor. Taking into account not only future population trends in cohort size, but also possible changes in economic growth and household formation, housing economist Thomas C. Marcin projected the demand for housing through 2030. He projected that total housing demand will continue at high levels during the 1980s. Then in the 1990s, regardless of assumptions about economic conditions, the demand for additional housing will drop because of the much smaller cohorts reaching their late twenties at that time.

How expensive or reasonable home prices will be, of course, depends on many forces other than population pressures—including interest rate levels and public policies about homeownership. As housing specialists George

Sternlieb and James W. Hughes have pointed out, housing affordability is largely determined by mortgage interest rates. And no one knows what home mortgage rates will be in the 1990s.

But if we assume that public policies will continue to encourage home-ownership, and that home loans will continue to be available, then the effect of population pressure alone on home prices can be reasonably projected. As a consequence of changing cohort sizes, home prices should become more reasonable (in real terms) from 1990 through 2000. People born in the late 1960s and early 1970s, like those born in the 1930s, should find themselves in a favorable period for buying their first homes. The other side of the coin is that older cohorts selling their homes in the 1990s may receive less for them than they would have if they sold them in the 1980s—once again, holding inflation constant. The housing construction business also can be expected to be more prosperous in the 1980s than it may be in the 1990s.

Becoming a homeowner is only one part of forming links with a locality. Now let us turn our attention to our second topic—the matter of staying put.

WHO IS MOST—AND LEAST—LIKELY TO CHANGE RESIDENCES?

The United States may be a nation of movers, but not everyone moves every year. And of those who do change addresses, some only move across the street or down the block. As we shall see, chances of moving largely depend on age, region of residence, and marriage and employment statuses. To distinguish movers from stayers, the Bureau of the Census asks the following question: "Was .... living in this house (apartment) one year ago?" Movers are defined as people who lived at a different residence one year ago.

State Differences in Residential Mobility

The people most likely to change addresses live in the western and southwestern states listed in the top half of Table 7-4. One-third or more of the entire populations of four states—Alaska, Nevada, Wyoming, and Colorado—changed addresses during the year before the 1980 census. Many of these movers were recent arrivals from other states. One-fifth or more of the populations of each of these four states lived in a different state five years before.

With so much geographic mobility in the western states, the ties of many people to a specific locality are short term. Large portions of local communities were born and raised in other states. A long-term resident of a community or neighborhood may be someone who moved in just ten or fifteen years before.

Table 7-4 Which States Had the Highest—and the Lowest—Rates of Residential Mobility in the United States in 1980?

State	Mobility Rate*	Percentage of Population that Lived in a Different State in 1975
HIGHEST RESIDENTIAL MOBILITY:		
1. Alaska.............	39%	29%
2. Nevada............	38%	32%
3. Wyoming	34%	28%
4. Colorado	33%	21%
5. Arizona...........	32%	24%
6. Oregon............	30%	17%
7. New Mexico	30%	17%
LOWEST RESIDENTIAL MOBILITY:		
1. Pennsylvania	16%	5%
2. New Jersey.........	17%	8%
3. New York..........	17%	4%
4. West Virginia	18%	9%
5. Connecticut	18%	9%
6. Massachusetts	18%	7%
7. Rhode Island	20%	9%

*Householders who moved into their homes during the twelve months preceding April 1, 1980, as a percentage of all householders.

Source: U.S. Bureau of the Census, *Statistical Abstract of the United States: 1984* (104th Ed.), Tables 16, 1341, pp. 16, 751.

If frequent moving, and many people arriving from other states, are characteristics of western states, the opposite is true for several eastern states. Those with the lowest levels of residential mobility are listed in the bottom half of Table 7-4. In Pennsylvania and New York, as examples, less than one-sixth of the population changed addresses during the year before the 1980 census, and only one-twentieth lived in a different state five years before. Many movers in eastern states went right out of the state and were not there to be counted in the census. Their destinations often were southern, southwestern, and western states, thus supplying those regions with large numbers of in-migrants.

With few people moving to eastern states, high proportions of the populations residing there are still living in the state in which they were born. They have long-term ties to their home states, and often to a specific locality. With only a small number of arrivals from other states, in some communities people who moved in during the past ten or fifteen years are still thought of as newcomers.

The geographic patterns of mobility tell us where the greatest activity is, and how population flows from one region of the nation to another. But they do not tell us why some people move, while others stay. To understand that we have to know something about the people themselves.

The Importance of Age for Residential Mobility

Who were the movers? According to a national survey of 58,000 households conducted by the Bureau of the Census in March, 1982, movers primarily were young adults. If you are in your early twenties, you are at the peak ages for moving. Nationally the odds are better than one in three that you changed your address during the past year (Table 7-5). You are more

Table 7-5 When Is the Transition to High Residential Mobility? To Low Mobility?
Percentage of People Who Changed Residences between March 1981 and March 1982 by Age and Gender

Age Group	Percentage Movers	
	Men	Women
ADOLESCENT TRANSITION:		
15–19 Years	13%	16%
HIGH RESIDENTIAL MOBILITY AGES:		
20–24 Years	33%	38%
25–29 Years	31%	29%
30–34 Years	22%	18%
MIDLIFE TRANSITION:		
35–44 Years	14%	12%
LOW RESIDENTIAL MOBILITY AGES:		
45–54 Years	9%	8%
55–64 Years	7%	6%
65–74 Years	5%	5%
75 Years and Over	4%	6%

Source: U.S. Bureau of the Census, "Geographic Mobility: March 1981 to March 1982," *Current Population Reports,* Series P-20, No. 384 (February 1984), Table 4, p. 14.

than twice as likely to move than you were in your late teens. Although some people begin settling down after their mid-twenties, many are still frequently changing residences in their early thirties.

Just as there is a marked conversion from low to high residential mobility during a person's late teens and early twenties, so is there a transition to low mobility during one's late thirties and early forties. If changing addresses frequently is a major part of the lives of young adults, then remaining at the same address for several years is a characteristic trait of older people. The contrasts are extreme, and, as Table 7-5 shows, highly related with age.

What explains such dramatic ups and downs with age in the chances of staying at the same place? Is it merely a matter of personal preference—that young people like moving frequently and older people do not? Is moving a goal for young adults, as homeownership is for most married couples, for which people strive? Or is it instead an activity people undertake as a means to attain goals, and, once having achieved them, they no longer have any reason to move?

Social demographers Gary D. Sandefur and Wilbur J. Scott have concluded that, as may be expected, moving is a means to an end and not an end in itself. They documented that the decline in geographic mobility with increasing age is almost completely explained by commitments to family activities and to employment. People change residences to achieve goals in the realms of family life and employment, and then settle down after they, their spouses, and their children develop ties in a community.

Exactly how do employment, marriage, and parenthood influence settling down? To answer that question let us consider the sexes separately. And let us also compare young adults in their late teens and early twenties (who are approaching the peak moving ages), with people in their late thirties and early forties (who are passing through the midlife transition for settling down).

Who Is Most Likely to Change Residences among Young Adults? A change of residence often accompanies a major life transition—graduating from high school or college, marrying or divorcing, or taking a new job. It is not surprising, then, that the most mobile young adults in 1982 were those who already had made some important life choices. The most mobile young men were those serving in the armed forces. They had chosen an occupation that required frequent changes in residence. Among the most mobile young women in 1982 were those who by age twenty-four had been both married and divorced—over half moved the year before.

If you are under twenty-five and married, you are more than twice as likely to move than are never-married people your same age. For many newly married couples, changing addresses frequently is seen as a natural part of the process of setting up a new life together. Childless householders especially change addresses frequently—over half moved in 1982. But the arrival of children slows things down. And once their children enter school, couples become even less likely to move.

One consequence of graduating from college, or of being young and having a high-paying job, is an increase in the likelihood of moving. The two often go together. The transition from student to full-time worker often requires a change of address. On graduating from college, or after completing a program of graduate education, you may find that the best-paying jobs often are not where you have gone to school. Between forty and forty-five percent of college graduates in their early twenties change their addresses each year. And the highest-paying jobs usually go to those willing to move as the job requires.

If you lose your job, you also are more likely to move. The consequent drop in income can force you to change your residence even against your wishes. The combination of being recently married and unemployed leads to unusually high levels of mobility among young adults. Two-thirds of the women in their late teens and early twenties who were in this situation changed residences in 1981. They were more than four times more mobile than women in the same age group who had never married and were not in the labor force (most of whom were still living at home with their parents, were full-time students, or both). A similar pattern prevailed among men of the same age, but with somewhat lower mobility rates. Over half of the unemployed, married young men moved the year before—four times the rate of never-married men who were not in the labor force.

Young adults least likely to be movers were those who had not yet made certain transitions—those who had never married, were not in the labor force, had little or no personal income, or had gone to college but had not yet graduated. If you are in any one of these situations, then chances are about one in four or less that you moved during the past year. When two or more transitions were yet to be made, people were even less likely to move. Young women who were both never married and not in the labor force in 1982, for example, were less mobile than either never-married young women (some of whom worked), or those not in the labor force (some of whom were married).

Who Is Least Likely to Move in Early Middle Age? The middle-aged people least likely to move are married, have good incomes, and own their own homes. They not only have achieved some of their major life goals, they also have developed ties to a local community through their family, job, and housing commitments. They see little reason to move.

Among the most settled people in early middle age, for example, are married couples. Their mobility rates are only one-fifth as large as those of married couples twenty years younger. It should be remembered that at this stage in life most people are, in fact, married and living with their spouses. Married people living with their spouses accounted for about three-quarters of all persons in their late thirties and early forties in 1982.

High-income middle-aged men and women also have low mobility rates. Their high incomes frequently result from years of working for the same company, or from having established themselves after years of effort in a particular neighborhood or territory. Occupations that depend greatly for success on developing a clientele in a given locality include private-practice lawyers and physicians, dentists, clinical psychologists and therapists, and insurance salespersons. For men and women employed in such careers, moving to a new location usually would mean starting over again at a lower level of income.

The effect on moving of having a college education is concentrated among people just starting out in life. By early middle age its influence has largely disappeared. Among people in their late thirties and early forties in 1982, for example, there was no difference for either gender in mobility rates between high-school graduates and college graduates. In both cases mobility rates were low—about one-quarter as large as those of young college graduates.

If marriage increases the odds of staying put for middle-aged people, then the breaking of those commitments through divorce or widowhood often leads to a change of residence. The mobility rates of previously married middle-aged men and women were two to three times higher than those of currently married people of the same age and gender in 1982.

When employment ties also have been broken, unusually high rates of mobility result. Middle-aged people who are both unmarried and unemployed find themselves once again in transition, much as they were twenty years earlier. They change addresses almost as frequently as do much younger people. Unemployed, previously married men and women in their late thirties and early forties in 1982 were almost four times more likely to have moved than were men and women the same age who were both employed and married.

Mobility rates decline steadily for men and women after their mid-forties (Table 7-5). The few older people who do change residences commonly do so, as would be expected, because of a major life transition. Older people most likely to move are those who are recently retired, or just widowed, or no longer able to live by themselves because of health problems.

Having settled down long ago, few older people are concerned about moving to a new address. Instead, they are much more interested in living stable and financially secure lives in retirement. Even though most no longer receive income from paid employment, they still must make ends meet. Unless you continue working until the day you die, eventually you will face the same situation. The following chapter provides information that can help you judge how your membership in a particular birth cohort may affect what you can expect in retirement.

8/

What Can You Expect in Retirement?

The Social Security system that improved the well-being of millions of retired people now suffers from a long-range population problem—the great size of the Baby Boom cohort. Some doubt whether people born during and after the Baby Boom will enjoy Social Security retirement benefits as good as those being paid to older people today. A growing political awareness of this potential flaw in the system led to the passage of the Social Security Amendments of 1983. In an attempt to restore financial soundness to the system, taxes were raised and, for some, benefits reduced. Wealthier retirees were required to pay income tax on some benefits that had been tax free. People who will be retiring before age sixty-five in the future will receive a lower level of support than was the case in the past.

Will these changes work? Will the Social Security system provide the same level of retirement support for people born after 1946 as it now does? Or will the Baby Boom and Baby Bust cohorts pay higher Social Security taxes through middle age, only to find that when they retire their benefits will be lower than those of their parents and grandparents?

There are no easy answers. The link between changing cohort sizes and the Social Security system is an example of how a large societal process can influence your personal well-being whether you are aware of it or not. By learning more about the situation, however, you may be able to arrange your own life so as to minimize the harmful effects on you of the Social Security system's problems.

This chapter's goal is to provide you with some of that information. It will show you how cohort analysis, used in earlier chapters, can be applied to judging what you can expect from Social Security. The financial aspect of retirement, of course, is only one of many important matters to consider for your later years. References cited for this chapter can introduce you to the wide range of issues that social gerontologists have studied concerning the elderly, including health prospects and access to health care, family life, transportation, housing, adult education, and civic involvement.

For our present purposes, however, we shall focus on the connection between population change and your financial well-being in your sixties and later. If the knowledge presented in this chapter makes you doubt your previous expectations about Social Security, then you may wish to consider alternative means of providing for your old age. Retirement planning is particularly important for women. Women not only can expect to live longer than men, they also can expect to receive less retirement income, on the average, than men. In spite of the special retirement problems of women, Lois B. Shaw reports that only half of working women in their early forties had made any plans about their retirement.

To help you make your own judgments about your need to plan for your retirement, this chapter will examine the following issues:

1. When, and how long, will your retirement be?
2. Population change and supporting the elderly.
3. What can you expect from Social Security?
4. Should you plan to be financially independent of Social Security? What would this require—now and later?

WHEN, AND HOW LONG, WILL YOUR RETIREMENT BE?

Some people your age will live into their nineties and spend thirty years or more in retirement. Who is to say that you will not be among them? Many people live much longer than they expected. Unfortunately, many also outlive their life savings. If you want to avoid outliving your personal retirement resources, you need to have some idea how long your retirement will be, and when it will be. With this knowledge, you can better prepare for your retirement while you are still employed (or married to someone who is).

Although no one can predict your individual life span, demographers can project what proportions of specific birth cohorts will reach certain ages. For example, over four-fifths of women born in 1968, and almost three-quarters of men born in the same year, will live to celebrate their sixty-fifth birthdays if the 1980 United States death rates remain unchanged. But the 1980 death rates almost certainly will be replaced with lower death rates (assuming no world war, or similar disaster). As the causes of death come under greater control, your chances become even better for living to age sixty-five and beyond.

If you were born before 1968, you are even more likely to reach age sixty-five than are people younger than yourself. You already have survived longer and are closer to reaching your sixty-fifth birthday. Paradoxically, the older you are, the longer your total life expectancy. An extreme example illustrates the process: people who have the best chances of living to be one hundred are those who had their ninety-ninth birthdays fifty-one weeks ago.

Because the odds favor your reaching age sixty-five, let us assume you do. What then? How many more years of life can you expect at that age?

The average remaining years of life at age sixty-five, for specific birth cohorts, have been calculated by the Social Security Administration. These estimates assume an increasingly greater control over death in future decades; thus life expectancy at age sixty-five gradually lengthens for younger cohorts. Results for selected cohorts are shown in Table 8-1. These are average life expectancies. Many people will live even longer if they watch their

Table 8-1 When, and How Long, Will Your Retirement Be?
Projected Average Remaining Years of Life at Sixty-Fifth Birthday by Gender for Selected Cohorts Born between 1920 and 1979

Birth Year	Sixty-Fifth Birthday In:		Average Remaining Years of Life		Retirement Period*	Total Life Expectancy
WOMEN:						
1920	1985	+	20.6	=	1985–2006	85.6 Years
1930	1995	+	21.2	=	1995–2016	86.2 Years
1940	2005	+	21.6	=	2005–2027	86.6 Years
1950	2015	+	22.1	=	2015–2037	87.1 Years
1960	2025	+	22.6	=	2025–2048	87.6 Years
1970	2035	+	23.1	=	2035–2058	88.1 Years
1979	2044	+	23.5	=	2044–2068	88.5 Years
MEN:						
1920	1985	+	15.7	=	1985–2001	80.7 Years
1930	1995	+	15.9	=	1995–2011	80.9 Years
1940	2005	+	16.3	=	2005–2021	81.3 Years
1950	2015	+	16.7	=	2015–2032	81.7 Years
1960	2025	+	17.0	=	2025–2042	82.0 Years
1970	2035	+	17.4	=	2035–2052	82.4 Years
1979	2044	+	17.7	=	2044–2062	82.7 Years
YOUR BIRTH YEAR:						
____	____	+	____	=	____–____	____Years

*Assuming retirement begins on sixty-fifth birthday.

Source: Joseph F. Faber and Alice H. Wade, "Life Tables for the United States: 1900–2050," *Actuarial Study No. 89* (December 1983), Office of the Actuary, Social Security Administration, SSA Pub. No. 11-11536, Table 7, pp. 77–78.

blood pressure, wear seat belts in automobiles, do not smoke, and do not drive after drinking.

We now have all the information we need to project when, and how long, your retirement will be. The younger your retirement age, of course, the longer your retirement period will be. If you retire at the presently customary age of sixty-five, then your birth year plus sixty-five gives you the year your retirement will begin. That year, plus your life expectancy at age sixty-five, shows your projected retirement period. If you were born in any turn-of-the-decade year between 1920 and 1979, I already have made these calculations for you in Table 8-1. If you were born in an in-between year, I have left a line in the table where you can easily calculate your own likely retirement period by using the "average remaining years of life" nearest your own birth year.

Generally speaking, the same picture emerges for all cohorts. If you are a woman, you should expect to live at least until your late eighties. If you retire in your mid-sixties, you would then spend over twenty years in retirement. If you are a man, you should plan on being retired for over sixteen years, and on seeing your eighty-first birthday.

As I mentioned, it is important for making life choices to know not only how long your retirement period will be, but also when it will occur. Much depends on whether it will be before, during, or after the Baby Boom's retirement period. Assuming retirement at age sixty-five, the first Baby Boom members (born in 1946) will begin retiring in 2011. Some of the last Baby Boom members, born in the early 1960s, will still be living in retirement after 2050. So we will examine two retirement periods—from the present to 2011, and from 2011 through 2050.

POPULATION CHANGE AND SUPPORTING THE ELDERLY

The younger population directly supports the older, retired population through gifts of goods and services. It also provides indirect support by paying taxes for public programs from which older persons benefit. The efforts of younger, employed people also make possible the returns on financial assets privately owned by older, retired people.

The transfer of wealth from younger to older generations creates a potential for conflict between the two age groups. Hostility rarely arises, however, because of a trade-off in social values accepted by both groups across the life course. Some believe that because parents provided for their children, grown children should, if need be, support their elderly parents. Many people are willing to pay taxes for programs that benefit the elderly (such as Social Security), out of a belief that no one should be allowed to fall below a certain minimum standard of living. And most people in the United States share common values about private property, and willingly pay owners—

regardless of their age—the rents, interest, etc., charged for the use of the property.

Open disagreements could develop, however, if the expectations of the receiving group exceed the ability, or the willingness, of the supplying group to provide. In either case, the numbers of people involved is important. Expectations for support can be too high if there are too many receiving people. Ability to supply can be insufficient if there are not enough providers. In terms of retirement prospects, this means comparing the sheer number of older, retired people with the number of younger adults.

A straightforward way to do this is to simply compare the number of people sixty-five and over with the number of people who are from twenty through sixty-four years old. The resulting figure is called the "support ratio." In 1980, the support ratio was one person sixty-five and over for every five people aged twenty through sixty-four. Not everyone sixty-five and over, of course, is retired. But most are. Among people of that age in 1981, for example, only one in ten women, and one in five men, were still in the labor force.

Support Ratios through 2050

How will the burden of supporting the elderly change in the future? In making their own projections of the support ratio, the Social Security Administration uses three sets of assumptions ranging from optimistic to pessimistic. (None of the three projections takes illegal immigration into account; thus all three understate the actual number of people who will be living in the United States.) I have listed their results in Table 8-2—both the total number of people sixty-five and over projected through 2050, and the corresponding support ratios.

A good way to read the table is to find the row with the birth cohort nearest your own. That row shows you what you can expect when you turn sixty-five. Look across that row to see how the burden of supporting the elderly varies according to the assumptions made in each of the three projections. Having done this, the next step would be to think about the retirement situations of people you know who are older or younger than you, maybe a relative, friend, or neighbor. Find the rows that come closest to their birth years, and compare the three projections. Because of the sudden rise in the number of older people after 2011, the retirement situation of people born during and after the Baby Boom will be quite different from that of those born before.

From now through 2000, for example, it does not much matter which projection you look at. The number of people sixty-five and over differs by only three million between the highest and lowest projections. The most rapid increase in the number of older people at that time will be among those seventy-five and older—caused by the greater proportions of people surviv-

Table 8-2 When Will the Size of the Older Population Suddenly Increase?
Projections of the Number of People Sixty-Five and Over in the Social Security Area of the United States, 1980 through 2050

Year	Birth Cohort Turning 65	Millions 65 and Over			Support Ratio*		
		I	II	III	I	II	III
BEFORE THE BABY BOOM COHORT RETIRES:							
1980	1915	26	26	26	20	20	20
1990	1925	32	33	33	21	22	22
2000	1935	35	36	38	21	22	23
2010	1945	38	41	44	21	23	25
AFTER THE BABY BOOM COHORT RETIRES:							
2020	1955	49	53	58	27	30	34
2030	1965	61	66	74	33	38	46
2040	1975	62	69	80	32	39	52
2050	1985	62	70	83	30	39	58

*Support Ratio = People 65 and over for every 100 people 20–64.
Projection I assumes: (1) fertility rises from 1.9 children per woman in 1985 to 2.3 children in 2007 and later; (2) life expectancies at birth increase by 3 percent between 1985 and 2040; and (3) an annual net immigration of 450,000.
Projection II assumes: (1) fertility rises slightly from 1.9 children per woman in 1985 to 2.0 children in 2000 and later; (2) life expectancies at birth increase by 6 percent between 1985 and 2040; and (3) an annual net immigration of 400,000.
Projection III assumes: (1) fertility declines from 1.8 children per woman in 1985 to 1.6 children in 2007 and later; (2) life expectancies at birth increase by 10 percent between 1985 and 2040; and (3) an annual net immigration of 350,000.

Source: John C. Wilkin, "Social Security Area Population Projections, 1983," *Actuarial Study No. 88* (August 1983), Social Security Administration, SSA Pub. No. 11-11535, Table 15, pp. 36–38.

ing into extreme old age. The support ratios also are much the same, and show only small increases from 1980 levels. (The age and sex compositions of the United States in 1985 and 2000 are illustrated in Figures 2-1 and 2-2 in Chapter Two.)

One reason for the modest increases in the support ratios is that the people retiring at that time will be members of the small Great Depression cohort. If you were born in the 1930s, your Social Security retirement expectations (at least through 2010), could be easily handled by the large number of Baby Boom members. The latter will be middle-aged, at their peak earning period in life, and paying large amounts of taxes into the system.

There is another reason for the similarity of the three projections in 2000—it is too soon for the different assumptions about births, deaths, and immigration to have had much, if any, effect. Everyone twenty and over in 2000 already has been born, so fertility assumptions are not yet relevant. The small differences in mortality and migration assumptions produce only small population differences in such a short period of time. The farther into the future the projections are made, however, the wider are the contrasts among them.

If you are among the first members of the Baby Boom cohort, you probably will have retired by 2020. Your number will have been added to a suddenly increasing number of older people. In the twenty years following 2010, the support ratio will increase from twenty-three to thirty-eight older people for every one hundred younger adults (in Projection II). Your cohort's expectations for retirement support will suddenly place heavier burdens on people younger than yourself.

You will be one of those supporting people if you were born after the mid-1960s. The small Baby Bust cohort of the late 1960s and 1970s will be middle-aged in 2020, squeezed between demands for support by their own children (and grandchildren), and their retired parents. If you are a member of the Baby Bust cohort, you will be directly faced with the problem of supporting the large, retired Baby Boom cohorts through tax-supported public programs such as Social Security.

If the Baby Bust cohort decides to solve the old-age support problem by reducing the benefits of the Baby Boom cohort, then they may be setting a precedent for their own retirement. Younger generations may follow their example, and change the benefits that retired people can expect. In 2040 the Baby Bust cohort members will be in their sixties and seventies: how many younger people will there be to support them? More than ever before, the answer depends on the assumptions made about births, deaths, and immigration.

Under the most optimistic set of assumptions (Projection I), the support ratio begins to improve (to decline) after 2030 because of the continuing growth of the younger population caused by higher fertility levels. The demographic crunch caused by the retirement of the Baby Boom would be passing. The burden of caring for them, and the Baby Bust cohort, would have been solved by having a much larger total population in the United States Social Security Area—380 million in 2050. That would be a 144 million increase from the 1980 size.

At the other extreme, the most pessimistic assumptions (Projection III) produce a seemingly unmanageable aged-dependency burden in 2020. The people who bore the greatest burden of supporting the Baby Boom cohort in its retirement, those born in 1965 and later, almost certainly would find their own retirement well-being in jeopardy. Because of the below-replacement levels of fertility, the total population would be declining in size after having peaked at 290 million in 2030. But the retired population would continue growing. By 2050 there would be almost six people sixty-five or older for every ten people between twenty and sixty-four years old.

So much for the extreme assumptions. What about the one the Social Security Administration considers most likely? The middle projection for 2030 through 2050 results in two people sixty-five and over for every five between the ages of twenty and sixty-four—an aged-dependency burden that would be almost double the level of 2000. In such a situation, the transfer of wealth from the younger to the older generations would require a much greater willingness to support retired people than is presently the case.

Figure 8-1 illustrates the change in support ratios between 2000 and 2040 (using the middle projection in both years). Notice the especially large increases in the sizes of the age groups seventy-five and over. They are caused both by the aging of the Baby Boom cohort (the oldest members of which will be ninety-four), and by the assumption of greater longevity. Also note how the middle-aged population will be smaller in 2040 than it was in 2000.

If the middle projection results in a doubling of the aged-dependency burden after 2000, what does that mean in terms of taxes and retirement benefits? Will taxes be raised? Or will benefits be cut? Or will both happen? What can your cohort expect in retirement benefits from the Social Security system?

WHAT ABOUT SOCIAL SECURITY?

As sociologists Judith Treas and Vern L. Bengston have described, widespread expectations about retiring at age sixty-five or earlier are relatively new. In 1940, for example, two-thirds of men sixty-five and over were still in the labor force. In those days fewer women worked outside the home. But when they did, more kept working after age sixty-five—one-eighth of all women over sixty-five were still working in 1940.

The withdrawal of older workers from the labor force since 1950, not only in the United States but in at least seventeen other nations as well, was primarily caused by technological and economic changes, according to the research of Fred C. Pampel and Jane A. Weiss. In the past, many older workers were employed in agricultural jobs, or in semiskilled and unskilled work. As nations became more highly urbanized, and as more jobs began requiring higher levels of training, fewer rural, unskilled, or semiskilled workers were needed. If older workers did not take up the new, more highly skilled occupations, or if they did not move to urban areas, they found themselves working fewer hours and even becoming unemployed.

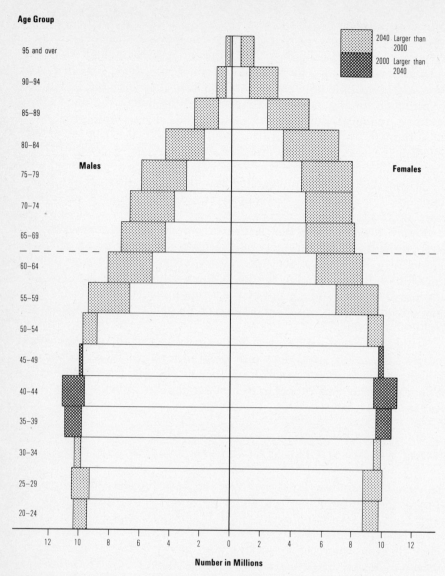

Figure 8-1 How Will the Number of People Sixty-Five and Over Change Between 2000 and 2040? Projected Population of the United States Social Security Area in 2000 and 2040 by Age and Sex.

Source: Alternative Projection II from John C. Wilkin, "Social Security Area Population Projections, 1983," *Actuarial Study No. 88* (August 1983), Social Security Administration, SSA Pub. No. 11-11535.

Pampel and Weiss also found that a less important, but still significant, explanation of the rise of widespread retirement was the amount of money spent for public programs for people sixty-five and over. Some of these programs originally were created during the Great Depression of the 1930s in response to the unemployment problems of older workers. In the United States that was the Social Security retirement program which began in 1940. Its original purpose had been merely to provide a supplementary income for some older workers who were no longer in the labor force. In 1955, for example, it paid benefits to only eight million retired workers and their survivors.

Many believe Social Security is a sort of insurance program for which they pay with "contributions" taken from their paychecks, with some extra money paid on their behalf by their employers. It is, in fact, a federal program for the aged, disabled, and their survivors, funded by taxes on some self-employed people and on payrolls—half paid by the employee and half paid by the employer. The Social Security system's financial reserves today are very small compared to its obligations. At the beginning of 1984, for example, Social Security's two major trust funds—the Old-Age and Survivors Insurance and Disability Insurance (OASDI) Trust Funds—only had enough money in them to pay less than three months' benefits in the absence of any income. By the 1980s, the Social Security system had become a pay-as-you-go program for transferring wealth from the working to the retired and disabled population.

By the 1980s, Social Security also had become a major source of income for tens of millions of people. In 1984, over one-seventh of the total United States population was receiving a monthly check from Social Security. Their numbers included twenty-six million retired people, four million disabled people, and seven million survivors of workers or disabled people. Between 1955 and 1984, the number of beneficiaries for every one hundred workers being taxed by the program increased from twelve to thirty-one.

As the numbers of older beneficiaries increased, so did political pressures to increase benefit levels. Older people are more likely to vote than are younger people. If we assume people vote for their own self-interests, as they perceive them to be, then many retired people will vote for political candidates who promise higher levels of old-age support. When the number of older voters grows faster than the rest of the population, the stage is set for more generous public programs benefiting older people. The increase in Social Security retirement benefit levels between 1940 and 1980 coincided with a near doubling in the ratio of people sixty-five and over to those aged twenty through sixty-four.

Because politics determines who pays how much in taxes, and who benefits from public programs, what you can expect from Social Security when you retire depends on how Congress and the President respond to the long-range problem of providing for the Baby Boom cohort's retirement.

Political Assumptions

The Social Security taxes workers pay reflect—through their elected representatives—their political willingness to support the program. Back in 1955, all of the Social Security tax went for the retirement program. In that year employees paid directly to Social Security a tax of two percent on earnings up to $4,200, in addition to the two percent paid by their employers. Thus in 1955 the combined payroll tax paid to Social Security was four percent. It is important to keep in mind that it is the combined payroll tax—and not just the half paid by employees—that pays most of the cost of the Social Security program.

After 1955 tax rates increased rapidly to support additional millions of beneficiaries, to increase levels of support, and to provide new programs. By 1984, employees and employers were paying a combined tax of fourteen percent on earnings up to $37,800. Of this amount, 10.4 percent went for the retirement program, 1.0 percent for the disability program, and 2.6 percent for the federal health program commonly called Medicare. Under current law the Social Security payroll tax will rise to 15.3 percent in 2000 and thereafter, including an 11.0 percent tax for the retirement program.

These tax rates have changed in the past, and may change again. Let us speculate about the willingness of taxpayers to support Social Security in the future. Let us first assume that taxpayers will continue paying whatever Social Security taxes are asked of them. Taxpayers may have grumbled a bit about the rising Social Security tax burden during the 1970s and early 1980s—but they paid. There was no taxpayers' revolt against Social Security taxes as there had been in some states against property taxes. There was no Social Security Reform Movement that tried to elect senators and representatives to Congress who promised to cut both taxes and benefits.

On the contrary, most taxpayers gave little thought to the Social Security system as a political issue. Sharing a general belief that benefits should be provided to older people, some taxpayers may have taken the system for granted. But retired people did not. Retired people's associations resisted reductions in current benefits, pressed for even higher benefit levels, and actively supported like-minded politicians. If this situation continues, then it seems reasonable to assume that Social Security will continue to provide expanding benefits for the currently retired, with Congress raising taxes whenever necessary. Although Congress has made slight revisions in Social Security benefits—including raising the normal retirement age for the Baby Boom and Baby Bust cohorts to sixty-six by 2009, and to sixty-seven by 2027, discouraging early retirement, and taxing some benefits received by certain wealthier retired people—it appears that no great change will be made in relieving the younger generation of the burden of paying for most of the program's cost.

Reasonable differences of opinion exist about the future political willingness of the younger population to support the older, retired population. Let us consider a pessimistic view. Let us assume that younger generations begin to take an interest in how much Social Security tax they pay, how the normal retirement age has been increased for their cohorts, and what retirement benefits they can expect. If you are a member of the Baby Boom or Baby Bust cohorts, for example, how do you think your agemates would feel about Social Security if the government announced that your agemates will receive a lower level of retirement support than that being provided the currently retired? Do you think they would be as willing to pay high Social Security taxes as they were before? Would they have as much confidence in the long-term fairness of the program?

If the Baby Boom cohort begins to doubt the system before the 1990s, then Social Security Reform could become a major domestic political issue. With the small 1930s cohort beginning to retire at that time, the voting power to change the system would rest with the large, middle-aged, Baby Boom cohort. The latter may decide to reduce benefits being paid in the 1990s to the level they expect to receive after 2011. Having voted to reduce Social Security taxes in the 1990s, however, the Baby Boom cohort could turn around and vote themselves increased benefits when they begin retiring after 2011. Their behavior would be consistent—they would merely be voting for their perceived self-interests at each stage in life, and using the political influence given them by their large numbers.

The willingness of the Baby Boom cohort to pay high taxes will depend in part on general economic conditions. They may pay higher taxes in good times, but balk at paying in bad times. Thus in addition to the demographic and political assumptions you make, the retirement benefits you can expect from the system also depend on your economic assumptions.

Economic Assumptions

As a starting point, let us consider the economic assumptions being made by the Social Security Administration itself. The law requires the administrators to make such economic assumptions each year when they estimate the financial soundness of the system. They arrange their economic assumptions in four alternative projections. So that you can decide for yourself which, if any, of these seems reasonable, we must examine the details. Fortunately the assumptions involve such straightforward matters as inflation, unemployment, the growth in the economy as measured by the real GNP (the Gross National Product), and the growth in the wages taxed by the Social Security system.

The most optimistic projection (top line in Table 8-3) assumes that inflation gradually declines to two percent a year by 1992, that the unemployment rate declines to five percent by 1990, and that growth will occur in the wages taxed by Social Security. It also assumes the most favorable demographic conditions (Projection I, described in Table 8-2). If this extremely

Table 8-3   How Much Will the Old-Age, Survivors, and Disability Insurance (OASDI) Programs of Social Security Cost in 2050?

Population Projection*	Economic Projection **	Beneficiaries per 100 Covered Workers	Cost of OASDI Programs***
I	A. Most Favorable	38	10.3%
II	B. Favorable	49	14.3%
II	C. Less Favorable	50	15.3%
III	D. Least Favorable	75	24.5%

*See Table 8-2 for assumptions underlying each population projection.
**See text for details of economic assumptions made.
***Cost of OASDI as a percentage of taxable payrolls.
Note: In 1984, the OASDI programs cost 11.3 percent of taxable payrolls, and there were thirty-one OASDI beneficiaries for every one hundred workers contributing to the program.

Source: U.S. Social Security Administration, *1984 Annual Report of the Board of Trustees of the Federal Old-Age and Survivors Insurance and Disability Insurance Trust Funds,* Washington, D.C. April 1984, Tables 29, 30, pp. 73–75.

optimistic view of the future materializes, then the cost of providing retirement and disability benefits for the Baby Boom cohort will remain below the twelve percent payroll tax scheduled by law. There will be no problem, and the retirement and disability program will not become a political issue.

But the Social Security administrators do not think such a rosy future is probable. They believe it is more reasonable to assume less favorable economic and demographic conditions. Their middle-range view is represented by two sets of economic assumptions applied to the "most likely" population projection (Projection II). One economic alternative assumes robust economic growth only slightly less favorable than in the all-out optimistic scenario. The other alternative assumes a lower economic growth in which inflation, for example, levels off at four percent a year from 1990 on, and the unemployment rate declines to six percent by 1991 and stays at that level.

Making these assumptions, the retirement and disability program costs are easily handled through 2015. Then, with increasing numbers of Baby Boom cohort members retiring, costs begin exceeding incomes. By 2030 over fifteen percent of the nation's payrolls would have to be taken in taxes each year to pay that year's Social Security retirement and disability benefits. Taxes also would be needed for the separate problem of paying for Medicare. In 2040, for example, when many Baby Bust cohort members will be retired, the total Social Security payroll tax would be 24.6 percent—15.2 percent for retirement and disability, and 9.4 percent for Medicare.

Social Security would try to meet these costs by drawing on any accumulated reserves it had at that time. But if the system continues on a pay-as-you-go basis, its reserves would be too small to matter. Benefits paid to the

Baby Boom and Baby Bust retirees would either have to be reduced, or Social Security taxes would have to be increased. The cost of Social Security could be managed by shifting national priorities away from other concerns, and by devoting a sizable share of the nation's wealth to programs benefiting the elderly.

The fourth, and most pessimistic projection, paints a dim future. The pessimism is primarily caused by the demographic conditions (Projection III), and not by the assumed economic prospects. I say this because, in my opinion, the economic conditions assumed by the Social Security administrators are only slightly worse than those for the middle projections. No recession is assumed; instead the economy continues to grow. Unemployment is projected to decline to seven percent by 2000, for example, and remain there. At the other extreme, no double-digit inflation is projected—at no time is inflation assumed to rise to over six percent a year over the next several decades. Such a golden age has not happened in the recent history of the United States. In 1980, for example, consumer prices increased by over thirteen percent. In 1982, the unemployment rate was almost ten percent.

Under the assumed good economic conditions, but less favorable demographic assumptions, the Social Security system faces major difficulties after the Baby Boom cohort begins retiring in 2011. Just to meet the costs of the retirement and disability program, the combined Social Security payroll taxes paid by employees and employers would have to rise from twelve percent paid in the late 1980s, to sixteen percent by 2020, and to over twenty-four percent by 2050 (bottom line in Table 8-3). In addition, Social Security would be collecting a tax of at least ten percent for Medicare, for a total Social Security payroll tax of thirty-four percent.

The system could be in danger of losing the political support of taxpayers long before tax rates ever reached that level. A major reform reducing benefits would be required to make the system financially sound. If you want more information about what the Social Security Administration is planning for your cohort's retirement period, you can write directly to them. Each year the system's trustees report on its current and long-term financial soundness. In your letter, simply ask for your own copy of the most recent "Annual Report of the Board of Trustees of the Federal Old-Age and Survivors Insurance and Disability Insurance Trust Funds." Single copies are free. The address to write to is listed in the references for this chapter.

The four official projections produced by the Social Security Administration, of course, do not cover all future possibilities. Critics would say, for example, that all of their projections assume much too optimistic economic conditions. Less favorable economic assumptions would result in even higher tax rates than officially projected, or important cuts in benefits paid, or both.

You may be willing to pay higher Social Security taxes, but others may not. Because the long-range consequences can be so important for you, why take a chance on shifts in the general public's willingness to support the aged after you have retired? Why not assume that most of your retirement income will come from your own resources—that Social Security will be for you, as it was originally intended, a supplement to your retirement? If so, what other resources will you have?

WILL YOU HAVE OTHER SOURCES OF FINANCIAL SUPPORT?

With few exceptions, your non-Social Security income after age sixty-five will come from your own initiative and efforts—both then and when you were younger. Judging by the situation of older people today, life savings will be particularly important. Two-thirds of people sixty-five and over in 1982, for example, received income in the form of interest on their savings or on loans they had made (Table 8-4). Assuming you have some income remaining after meeting your living expenses, how much of it you will have saved by the time you retire is largely up to you. You may be able to increase the amount saved by maintaining a simpler life style, including resisting advertising and peer-group pressures to buy things on credit. The trade-off is between lower consumption today and greater financial security later. Which do you value more?

While most older people had some savings in 1982, only a minority had any income from the third most common source of income—dividends, rent, or income from estates or trusts. Sociologist Robert C. Atchley has pointed out the difficulty most working people have in saving and investing for their retirement. Does this mean that the odds are against your having any investments paying dividends or rents after you retire? Not necessarily. As we have seen in Chapter Three, your income should be better than average if you are college educated, and especially if you are married and both you and your spouse work in full-time, year-round jobs. If you are able to save some money each year for your retirement, you could invest your savings so as to earn dividends, rent, or capital gains instead of just earning interest. One word of caution—I believe you should be willing to invest your time, as well as your money, and learn how to invest wisely.

You have one advantage in investing that currently retired people did not have when they were young. The federal government now encourages people to set up tax-deferred Individual Retirement Accounts (IRAs). The Internal Revenue Service permits you to deduct your contributions to your IRA investment from your taxable income (up to $2,000 a year). In addition, taxes on any income earned by the IRA, or any increase in its value, are deferred until after you retire.

The resulting tax-deferred growth in worth can be impressive. Let us assume, for example, that you invested $2,000 a year in an IRA starting at age twenty-nine, and that your IRA earned twelve percent a year. Thirty years later your $60,000 investment would have grown to over $540,000. Thirty years of systematic, tax-deferred investing may seem like eternity.

Table 8-4   Where Do Older People Obtain Their Income?
Type of Income Received by People Aged Sixty-Five Years and Over
in 1982, by Gender

| | Percent Receiving Income | | |
Type of Income	Men	Women	Total
MOST COMMON SOURCES:			
1. Social Security or Railroad Retirement	90%	91%	91%
2. Interest on Savings, etc.	70%	64%	67%
LESS COMMON SOURCES:			
3. Dividends, Rents, Estates, and Trusts .	26%	21%	23%
4. Private Pensions or Annuities	28%	10%	18%
5. Wage or Salary Income	17%	9%	12%
6. Supplemental Security Income	4%	8%	6%
7. State or Local Employee Pensions . . .	5%	6%	6%
LEAST COMMON SOURCES:			
8. Veterans' Payment Income	5%	2%	3%
9. Federal Employee Pensions	4%	2%	3%
10. Nonfarm Self-Employment Income . .	5%	1%	3%
11. Miscellaneous Income Sources	3%	2%	3%
12. Farm Self-Employment Income	2%	*	1%
13. Worker's Compensation Income	*	*	*
14. Military Retirement Pensions	1%	*	*
15. Public Assistance or Welfare Income	*	*	*
16. Unemployment Compensation Income	*	*	*
No Income	*	2%	1%
Thousands of People 65 and Over . .	10,516	15,222	25,738

*Less than one percent had any income from this source.
Note: Many people have more than one source of income.

Source: Bureau of the Census, "Money Income of Households, Families, and
Persons in the United States, 1982," *Current Population Reports* (February
1984), Series P-60, No. 142, Tables 45, 50, pp. 144, 172, 174.

But thirty years without saving and investing is just as long, and produces no
nest egg in the end.

The fourth-ranking source of income for older people is a private pension
or income from a life insurance annuity. Among currently retired people,
men are much more likely to have private pensions than are women. If you
are a young woman, does that mean you are less likely to have a pension after
you retire than a young man your same age? Not necessarily. It depends on

your goals for, and choices about, working full time and year-round for the same employer for several years. (Some unions also provide pensions for members of long standing.) Generally speaking, if you do not have such a work history you will not have a pension. It is in your interest to ask about company pension plans when making employment decisions—even for your first full-time job. It is important to know who is eligible for a pension, how the pension plan is funded, and whether retirement benefits are adjusted for inflation.

Some older people receive public employee pensions. Of all people sixty-five and over in 1982, for example, six percent had earned a pension from a state or local government, and three percent received monthly employee retirement checks from the federal government (aside from veterans or military retirement programs). Public pensions, like private pensions, usually are based on a combination of years of service and wages or salary earned.

The fifth most common source of income for older people in 1982 was wages and salaries earned as employees. In addition, some older people earned self-employment income. In spite of the growing popularity in recent years of early retirement, some men and women keep on working into their late sixties, seventies, and even beyond. They may shift from full-time to part-time employment, earn less than before, or work in an occupation different from the one they followed when younger, but they keep working. The rewards are many, including: (1) additional income; (2) intrinsic interest in the work itself; (3) social contacts made on the job; and (4) the social status and personal identity the job may provide.

Assuming your health holds up, you will have the same choice to keep working in your later years of life. You may be forced to retire from a particular job or career at sixty-five, sixty-eight, seventy, or whatever. But no one can force you to retire from all paid employment at any age.

You may not be familiar with the sixth most common source of income for older people—the Supplemental Security Income Program of the federal government. The intent of the program is to provide an income source of the last resort for impoverished aged, blind, and disabled people who are not able to provide a certain minimum level of living for themselves. The program began in 1974, is administered by the Social Security Administration, and is funded from the general revenues of the United States. The elderly poor are primarily female, once again reflecting the special retirement problems of women. In 1982, for example, one-twelfth of all older women, but only one-twenty-fifth of all older men received income from this special program for the poor.

How Much Are Older Peoples' Income Sources Worth?

Let us assume that you will have several sources of retirement income—including interest, dividends, or rents from your savings and investments;

your monthly Social Security checks; and perhaps a pension. Generally speaking, the more sources of income you have after you retire the better off you are. With multiple sources, if one does not work out as well as you expected then you can fall back on the others.

What can you expect to receive from the various sources? The dollar amounts no doubt will be different when you retire. Let us assume, nevertheless, that the overall ranking of the sources' relative worth will be about as it is today. To help you see which source provides the best income, I have listed the ten most common income sources of older people in 1982 according to their median incomes for men, and have calculated the gender gap in income for each source (see Table 8-5). The advantage of men over women in retirement income should narrow in the future because of: (1) the growing equalization of the sexes in many occupations; (2) less pay discrimination against women; and (3) more women working full time and year-round.

Monthly Social Security retirement checks may be the most common source of income among older people, but they rank eighth in dollar worth.

Table 8-5 How Much Are Older Peoples' Income Sources Worth?
Median Income from Selected Sources Received by People Aged Sixty-Five Years and Over in 1982, by Gender

	Median Income Received		Gender
Type of Income	Men	Women	Gap*
SOURCES WORTH THE MOST:			
1. Federal Employee Pensions	$18,000	$11,500	64%
2. Wage or Salary Income	$15,500	$10,100	65%
3. Dividends, Rents, Estates, and Trusts	$15,400	$ 9,700	63%
4. Nonfarm Self-Employment Income	$14,200	$ 8,200	58%
SOURCES WITH MIDDLE-RANGE WORTH:			
5. State or Local Employee Pensions	$12,500	$10,600	85%
6. Private Pensions or Annuities	$11,800	$ 8,500	72%
7. Interest on Savings, etc.	$11,500	$ 6,700	58%
SOURCES WORTH THE LEAST:			
8. Social Security or Railroad Retirement	$ 8,900	$ 5,400	61%
9. Veterans' Payment Income	$ 7,400	$ 4,900	66%
10. Supplemental Security Income	$ 3,800	$ 3,600	95%

*"Gender Gap" = Women's income as percent of males'.
Note: "Median" means middle. Of people receiving income from the source, half received more than the median, and half received less.

Source: Bureau of the Census, "Money Income of Households, Families, and Persons in the United States, 1982," *Current Population Reports* (February 1984), Series P-60, No. 142, Table 50, pp. 173, 175.

In 1982 Social Security provided a median retirement income of $8,900 for men and $5,400 for women. The lower figure for women was due in part to eligibility rules that favored people who had been full-time workers over those who had been part-time workers or full-time homemakers.

If you are, or plan to become, a long-term federal employee, you can look forward to a generous pension program—that is, assuming current federal employee retirement policies persist. In 1982, for example, the single most valuable income source for retired men and women was a federal employee pension. For men the average federal pension was worth $5,500 a year more than the average state or local government pension, and $6,200 more than the average private pension. If you are a woman, you also can expect a federal pension to pay more than other pensions, but the differences probably will be less. Among women the dollar advantage of the federal employee pension was $900 in 1982 over state or local government pensions, and $3,000 over private pensions.

A gender gap in income prevailed for all three pension sources. It was greatest for federal pensions, and least for state and local government pensions. Once again, the lower pension income received by women was due in part to gender differences in past earnings and in work histories. Even so, after federal pensions, the second most valuable source of retirement income for women in 1982 was a pension from a state or local government.

The third most valuable income source for older women (and second for men), were monies earned working as an employee. What this means is that the income benefits from working after your sixty-fifth birthday are real. An extra $5,000 can make a great difference in a retired person's financial well-being and independence. And the average income earned by older working people in 1982 was much more than $5,000. It was over $15,000 in wages and salaries for men, and over $10,000 for women. Self-employed people earned somewhat less—over $14,000 for men, and over $8,000 for women.

Income in the form of dividends or rents was one of the most valuable financial resources for both genders, producing almost as much income as earnings from wages and salaries. Interest earned on savings and loans was a somewhat less valuable source, but it was still worth more than Social Security retirement checks. The amount earned by women in interest, dividends, or rent was less than two-thirds that earned by men. Assuming both sexes invested equally wisely before and after retirement, then the lower earnings of women would have been caused by their having less to invest. This, in turn, could have resulted from the lower life-time earnings of women than men.

What is the overall retirement situation? First, you may well live far longer in retirement than you expect. Second, the Baby Boom cohort almost certainly will create major retirement problems for the federal Social Security system. Third, the less confidence you have in the dollar worth of Social Security benefits for your own retirement, the more seriously you may want to consider other retirement options while you are still young. (Retirement planning guides are helpful, such as the one published by the National Association of Mature People—listed in this chapter's references.) And fourth, the basic alternatives you have for paying for your own retirement are: (1) choosing an occupation, and working in a full-time, year-round job that permits you to earn a pension; (2) consuming less to save more for your retirement nest egg from the very beginning of your working years; and (3) working into your seventies, perhaps part time, hopefully in a job you find interesting.

9/

Making Choices in an Age of Uncertainty

At the start of this book I promised to take you on a journey through some major choices you will make during your life. Now the time has come to look back and review the ground we have covered.

Throughout, the book makes the "barring catastrophe" assumption—that economic depression, nuclear war, environmental breakdown, or epidemic disease will not happen. Each is possible, as pointed out in some of the references for this chapter. A prudent person considers such possibilities when making life choices. The potential of such events happening, however, should neither freeze a person into inaction at one extreme, nor prompt impulsive behavior at the other extreme. We may live in an age of uncertainty, but life goes on nevertheless. Choices must be made, and personal actions do have consequences.

The book also accepts the "knowledge is power" assumption. Knowing what to expect can help you make your own choices. This does not mean being able to forecast what will happen—the future is unknowable in detail. Instead, it means making reasonable projections about the future based on certain stated assumptions. Projections allow you to ask yourself what may happen to you if certain trends or events materialize. Population projections are especially useful for this purpose. They can give you information about questions directly connected to the choices you are making. They also are based on straightforward and easily understood assumptions.

The use of projections illustrates the third underlying assumption of this book—that one should take a future-oriented approach toward life. Having goals, and knowing where you want to be in twenty or thirty years, helps you get there. This is as true today as it was in the past. What is different today, however, is the rate of technological and social change. Life is more uncertain because the pace of change is more rapid.

I believe you can better cope with rapid change by becoming more self-directing. Self-directing people are willing to rethink not only the choices they are planning to make, but also the decisions they have made by now. They may decide to make different choices in the future. Or they may decide to change their expectations about past decisions. Although their decisions usually are similar to those made by most people their same age, self-directing people sometimes pay a price for being different from the crowd. That is what makes it such a difficult way to live.

Only you can decide how self-directing you will be—when you will go along with social pressures, and when you will not. As sociologist Peter L. Berger has pointed out, many people have more freedom to be self-directing than they realize. Their power of choice means that their lives are not entirely determined by "society" or some mix of "social forces."

A good way to decide when to conform is to use the sociological perspective to learn more about social pressures themselves. Sociology can show you the social importance of your own characteristics—including your gender, age, race, marital status, educational background, income, or employment status. It can improve your understanding of social values prevailing in the United States. It can describe how all of us can conform to many dominant social customs and yet remain distinct individuals. Only you, however, can decide the values by which you are going to organize your life. The personal questionnaires used throughout this book can help you identify and articulate your own values about jobs, marriage, sexual ideologies, parenting, and homeowning.

The factual information provided in this book shows you how other people in the United States have made, and may make, their decisions. For example, most men and women will work in the labor force, marry, become parents, and if they are married while middle-aged, be homeowners. They do these things either because they accept the values underlying their actions, or because they conform to gain rewards and avoid penalties. Let us assume the actions of the majority reveal an underlying script being lived out—a scenario written for them by the values, social institutions, and societal processes of their society. The higher the proportions of people doing the same things, presumably the greater the agreement on values, and the more intense the social pressures to conform. Actions of the minority who do not conform reveal the alternatives to following the script.

Which social roles and statuses do you expect to have in your own life script? Questionnaire F can help you answer that question. It lists many of the important life choices discussed in this book as a series of alternatives, and leaves spaces for you to indicate what you think your own situation will be in 1990, and twenty-five and fifty years from then. In thinking about your expectations, you may wish to review the chapters that discuss certain life

QUESTIONNAIRE F: **Which of the Following Social Roles and Statuses Do You Expect to Have in Your Life Script?**

In the space next to each year, write how old you will be at that time. Next, place a checkmark to indicate what social roles and statuses you expect to have in 1990, twenty-five, and fifty years later (discussions of the roles and statuses listed are found in sections of the Chapters indicated). Notice which roles and statuses, once attained, you expect to continue unchanged, and which you expect to vary across your life course.

Social Roles and Statuses I Expect To Have at Each Age:	*My Age In:*		
	1990: _____	2015: _____	2040: _____

EDUCATION (CHAPTER 3):

	1990	2015	2040
High-School Graduate	_____	_____	_____
Two-Year College Graduate	_____	_____	_____
Four-Year College Graduate	_____	_____	_____
Have a Master's or Professional Degree	_____	_____	_____

EMPLOYMENT (CHAPTERS 3, 4, 7, 8):

Not Yet in Labor Force	_____	_____	_____
Part-Time Worker	_____	_____	_____
Full-Time Worker	_____	_____	_____
Retired from Labor Force	_____	_____	_____

MARRIAGE (CHAPTERS 4, 5, 6, 7, 8):

Never Married	_____	_____	_____
Married (or Remarried)	_____	_____	_____
Divorced	_____	_____	_____
Widowed	_____	_____	_____

(Continued on Following Page.)

(Questionnaire F Continued.)

Social Roles and Statuses I Expect To Have at Each Age:	My Age In: 1990: _____	2015: _____	2040: _____
PARENTHOOD (CHAPTERS 5, 6, 8):			
Childless	_____	_____	_____
Parent	_____	_____	_____
Parent-in-Law	_____	_____	_____
Grandparent	_____	_____	_____
LIVING ARRANGEMENTS (CHAPTERS 5 & 6):			
Alone	_____	_____	_____
With Nonrelative(s)	_____	_____	_____
With Spouse Only	_____	_____	_____
With Spouse and Children	_____	_____	_____
With Children Only	_____	_____	_____
With Relatives Other Than Spouse or Children	_____	_____	_____
COMMUNITY LIFE AND RESIDENCE (CHAPTER 7):			
Changing Addresses Frequently	_____	_____	_____
Renter	_____	_____	_____
Homeowner	_____	_____	_____
Long-Term Resident in a Certain Locality	_____	_____	_____

choices. In filling out the questionnaire, please keep two important considerations in mind. First, the population-linked topics covered in this book are only fragments of the total script. They are important parts, nevertheless, because they are connected so tightly to much of the rest of our lives. Second, no one can predict the future—but you can be prepared for it.

You may find it easier to think about your life script after following one particular birth cohort through its life. Let us take people born in 1968 as our example. The following scenario is not a forecast of what will happen to the 1968 cohort. It is merely a projection of what may happen to them if certain trends materialize.

If you were born a year or two before or after the 1968 cohort, your life course will resemble its. Each birth cohort does have its own unique history, of course. But a year or two difference usually does not matter that much because population trends change slowly. The greater the age-gap between your cohort and the 1968 cohort, however, the greater the differences can become. If you were born before the late 1960s, the decisions made by your cohort almost certainly will differ in detail from those made by the 1968 cohort. But because the basic choices themselves do not change, a description of the 1968 cohort's life scenario still can help you better understand your own life course.

FRAGMENTS OF THE 1968 BIRTH COHORT'S LIFE SCRIPT

If you were born in 1968, you are among the first members of the Baby Bust cohort. There were eighteen percent fewer babies born in 1968 than in 1961. Your 1968 cohort was followed by even smaller birth cohorts. Birth rates kept falling and reached a low ebb during the mid-1970s. Then the number of births began to increase. By the early 1980s the Baby Bust was over. The Eighties Babies are, for the most part, the children of parents born during the Baby Boom.

Thus members of your Baby Bust cohort of the late 1960s and 1970s are in short supply. In this respect your cohort is similar to the small cohort born during the Great Depression of the 1930s. For most things in life, you and your Baby Bust associates picked a good time to be born. As a member of a small cohort, you will face less competition from your agemates than will the members of the Baby Boom cohort. The differences in cohort size almost certainly will persist throughout the lifetimes of the people involved.

1970s—Two through Eleven Years Old

Even though you were unaware of it during your first eleven years of life, you already were benefiting from your birth cohort's small size. In money spent, student-teacher ratios, and formal credentials of teachers, the educational system provided for your 1968 cohort was much better than that available to the first members of the Baby Boom cohort. If you went to a public school, you were taking advantage of a tax-supported service that had been greatly expanded during the 1960s and 1970s to cope with the demands of the large Baby Boom cohort. By the time your 1968 cohort was in sixth grade in 1980, for example, the amount of money being spent on each pupil in public schools had doubled since 1960 (holding inflation constant).

1980s—Twelve through Twenty-One Years Old

Educational Opportunities. Your improved educational opportunities continued through high school and college. Partly because the opportunities were there, you probably experienced strong social pressures to make the most of them. If your school was average, three-quarters or more of your fifth-grade classmates graduated from high school in 1986. Of those high-school graduates, over half began taking courses to earn a two- or a four-year college degree. Even though some will have left after one or two years, by the time your 1968 cohort turns twenty in 1988, between one-quarter to one-third are expected to be full-time or part-time college students.

Employment Prospects and Educational Choices. In recent decades changes in the job market have increased social pressures to complete a four-year college degree. Forty years ago many successful people never attended college, let alone graduated from one. Today some unusually talented (or lucky) people still do succeed without a college degree. But they are exceptions. Most people will improve their chances for success on the job by completing a four-year college degree, and especially so by going on to earn a Master's or a professional degree. This is true because many employed people older than you already have achieved such levels of education. They have developed high standards concerning educational qualifications needed to begin many careers.

Let us take people born in the mid-1950s as an example. That cohort was in its late twenties in 1982. Among those who were full-time, year-round workers, half had had some college, and one-quarter were college graduates. The proportions going to college, and graduating from college, were slightly higher for women workers than for men workers. With so many employed people having some college education, what would it take for you to stand out educationally from the crowd? If the same patterns persist for your 1968 cohort, when you are in your late twenties you would need a Master's or equivalent professional degree to rank in the upper tenth of your employed agemates.

Educational Choices and Income. Many people measure occupational success by how much money a person earns. If you happen to share this value, one attraction of achieving higher education is improving your chances for earning a higher income. Men and women, blacks and whites, all gain more income with higher education. While men gain more dollars with higher education, women make greater percentage gains in income—comparing college graduates with high-school graduates of the same sex. If you are a woman, what this means is that a college education is more important for you than it is for men if you want to have a higher income.

Competing in a high-paying and demanding career is a major life commitment. Even if you have the ability and the opportunity, you may choose not to conform to this particular expectation. If so, you would have one less reason for earning a four-year college degree. The trade-off is between having more time for your family, friends, and your own personal interests, and probably having a lower lifetime income.

1990s—Twenty-Two through Thirty-One Years Old

Your twenties will present you with major life choices about your occupation, marriage, and parenthood. The precise sequence of events may be different in your case than the average. You may have married and had children while still in your teens, for example. The point, though, is that the options are limited and that you cannot avoid making decisions about them. You are either in the labor force (full time or part time) or you are not. You are either never-married, married, divorced, separated, or widowed. You either are a parent or you are not. Let us take each fragment of the life script separately.

Employment Expectations. If you are a man, the social pressures to be employed by your early twenties are so intense that they point to only one socially acceptable alternative—continuing as a full-time student. Most young men will choose employment. If the labor force participation rates of the early 1980s persist through 1990, almost nine-tenths of men in their early twenties will be in the labor force, working or seeking work either on a full-time or a part-time basis.

If you are a woman you will have somewhat more freedom of choice about working in your early twenties. You will have essentially three alternatives to full-time, paid employment—continuing as a full-time student, becoming a full-time homemaker, or combining either (or both) of those roles with part-time employment. The expectations for you to have either a full-time or a part-time job will be strong. If the 1980s patterns persist, seven-tenths of women born in 1968 will be in the labor force by the early 1990s.

Pressures to be employed will increase during your mid and late twenties. When you are twenty-seven in 1995, almost all (ninety-four percent) of your male agemates will be in the labor force. More than eight-tenths of your female cohort members—regardless of their marital status—also will have jobs or be looking for paid employment. This projection assumes more women will be working in the 1990s than was the case in 1980. At that time two-thirds of women in their late twenties were in the labor force.

Occupational Choice. Assuming you will want to be employed, the chances are good that you will face less competition for your first full-time job than did people who were born at the peak of the Baby Boom (between 1957 and 1961). Because your cohort is being followed by even smaller cohorts, however, your job prospects in occupations serving people younger than yourself may be no better than those of the Baby Boom members. You may want to consider a career (such as a health field) serving people ten or twenty years older than yourself. In this way you could benefit from the large number of people passing through life just ahead of you.

In making your job choice, I believe you would be wise to take into account both the size of an occupation and its projected growth. Chapter Four describes several occupations that are growing rapidly through the late 1980s (and some growing only slowly or even declining). It also lists sources you can consult to keep up with changes in job prospects during the 1990s. One.trend to watch closely is the possibility of a computerized robot doing work similar to that which you are planning for yourself. Employment prospects for humans could be declining in some occupations even as the demand for the work itself increases.

But more important than such trends is the match between what you want from a job and what the job itself demands of you. You may want to "step outside yourself" and view your occupational values objectively. The questionnaire about occupational values presented in Chapter Four can help you begin doing this.

Having become more aware of what you want from a job, you may want to ask yourself if your job values result primarily from your own individual interests, abilities, and goals. Or do your job values result from traditional thinking about occupations in terms of sexual stereotypes? If so, you should know how the sexual stereotyping of some occupations is changing. If current trends persist, by the 1990s many traditionally male white-collar jobs will have higher proportions of women working in them. But occupations dominated by women, and male blue-collar jobs may be only slightly less sex-typed in the future than they are today.

Marriage Expectations. By 1995 you will be several years beyond the average age at first marriage. What can you expect about social pressures for being married by then? Given our assumption that the majority's actions reveal the underlying life script, being married still will be the expected way of life for people in their late twenties.

In spite of these expectations, you will have more choice about being married in 1995 than did people who were born in the mid-1950s and were in their late twenties in 1980. This will be especially true for men. The proportion married among all men in their late twenties is projected to decline from almost two-thirds to just over half between 1980 and 1995. Social pressures on women to be married are higher and will decline only slightly from current levels. Over two-thirds of women in their late twenties in 1995 are projected to be married, many to older men.

Marriage Alternatives. You will have just two alternatives to the marriage expectation—being never-married, or remaining unmarried after divorce or widowhood. Both options are projected to become more commonplace, and presumably more socially acceptable. You may well have never married by your late twenties, especially if you are a man. The Social Security Administration is projecting that two-fifths of men in your 1968 cohort, and one-fifth of women, will still be postponing marriage in 1995. At that time, never-married people will outnumber the divorced or widowed in your cohort.

Such projections help us know what other people your age may be doing in the future. But they do not tell us why they will be choosing to be married or unmarried. Sociologists assume most people who marry do so to achieve certain goals, and that many of those who remain unmarried want to realize different objectives. Marriage values and sexual ideologies may continue to change during the 1990s as they did during the 1970s and 1980s. In such times of rapid change, a person's own values can become confused. In the long run, I believe you are better off deciding for yourself by which values you will organize your family life, and your sexuality. The questionnaires included in Chapter Five can help you think about your own current marriage values and single values, and about your sexual ideology. Becoming more aware of your own values can improve your ability to communicate with your potential spouse, should you choose to marry. It may be more pragmatic than romantic, but your chances of having the marriage you want are improved if you and your potential spouse discuss what you each expect from marriage.

Parenthood Choices.   Assuming the peak age for giving birth continues to be a woman's late twenties, during the mid and late 1990s many 1968 cohort members will be making decisions about having children. If you have chosen to be married at that time, chances are that you also eventually will want to become a parent—most married people do. Less than one-twentieth of young wives in 1980, for example, said they never expected to become mothers.

From a life-course perspective, parenthood is much more a matter of raising children than of giving birth to them. Your parenting values, just as your marriage or other values, can change over time. But unlike marriage and other reversible life choices, parenthood is permanent—once a parent, always a parent. By becoming a parent you are taking on a major commitment to someone who had no say about becoming your child. The questionnaire included in Chapter Six can help you clarify your current thoughts about becoming a parent or not having children.

Your other life choices will influence your parenthood choices—both whether to become a parent and, if so, the number of children to have. The women most likely to remain voluntarily childless, or to have only one child, for example, are those with attractive alternatives to motherhood. If you are a woman who has completed, or plans to complete, five or more years of college, for example, you are among those least likely to become mothers. One reason is that postgraduate education can lead to life-long and well-paying careers such as administrators, managers, or professionals. On the other hand, the women most likely to have more than two children will be those who are not in the labor force, or who did not finish high school.

Living Arrangement Options. Your choices about marriage and parenthood will determine with whom who you will be living. Although the reasons behind your marriage and parenthood choices can be complex, your options about with whom to live are not. Everyone has only four choices—alone, with a nonrelative or nonrelatives, in a family, or in an institution. You can make that five choices, if you wish, by dividing family households into married-couple families on one hand, and all other combinations of relatives living together, on the other hand.

In which household type can you expect to be living in the mid-1990s? The social pressures to live in a married-couple family will be less then, according to assumptions made by the Census Bureau. The odds of living as a spouse in a husband/wife family in 1995 will be slightly less than fifty-fifty among people in their late twenties or early thirties.

Your main alternative to the husband/wife household will be living alone. More people postponing marriage results in more people living alone. What this means in personal terms is that a decision to postpone marriage usually is also a decision to live alone. Some unmarried, childless men and women will be living together in 1995, but they are projected to account for only a small fraction of all unmarried people.

Aside from living alone, the other main alternative to the husband/wife household at this stage in life will be living as a single parent with your children. This option will be primarily taken by women, given the Census Bureau assumption that nine-tenths of nonmarried-couple family heads in their twenties in 1995 will be women. Some of these mothers will have become parents without ever having married. About half will be mothers who are divorced and not remarried (assuming the early 1980s patterns persist). This type of family arrangement could account for one-sixth of the householders in your cohort in 1995.

2000 to 2014—Thirty-Two through Forty-Six Years Old

Community Life and Residence. Most married couples in their thirties and forties are making decisions about living in a particular locality for several years at a time, and becoming involved in a community—including becoming a homeowner. Although most people over thirty-five would like to own their own homes, you may prefer renting. The questionnaire in Chapter Seven can help you see how strongly you may hold homeowning values or renting values.

The values of the people with whom you will be living, of course, also will influence whether you own or rent. Thus your choices about marriage and parenthood have consequences for your housing expectations and opportunities. If you have never married and are living alone in your late thirties and early forties, the odds are four-in-five that you will be a renter—

assuming early 1980s patterns persist. If you are unmarried and living with relatives (a single parent, for example), chances are you still will be a renter.

Homeowning Prospects. If you are married and in your late thirties and early forties, the odds of your being a homeowner should be better than two-in-three. Whether you are white, black, or Hispanic, you can increase your homeowning prospects in three ways. First, choose to have both your spouse and yourself working in full-time, year-round jobs. Second, move away from certain large cities (listed in Chapter Seven), where renting is a way of life. And third, postpone having any children until after buying your first home. Married couples without children outnumbered those with children by four to three among first-home buyers in 1980.

As a member of a small cohort, your prospects for buying your first home in your late twenties or early thirties should be better than were those of the Baby Boom cohort back in the late 1970s and early 1980s. Based on the sheer numbers of people reaching the peak first-home buying stage in life, there should be less competition to buy a first home in the late 1990s than at any time during the previous twenty years.

Expectations to Settle in One Location. Becoming a homeowner is one aspect of putting down roots in one location. By your thirties and early forties you almost certainly will be moving less frequently than you did in your twenties. The reason for this change in lifestyle will be the commitments you will have made through your employment, marriage, and parenthood choices. Your commitments tie you more closely to one location.

The most mobile of your agemates at this stage in life will be those whose job or family ties have been broken—the unemployed or the divorced. The Social Security Administration is projecting that one-tenth of the 1968 cohort will be divorced and not remarried in the year 2000. The mobility rates of people in their thirties and forties who are both unemployed and divorced approach those of people ten or twenty years younger because they find their lives in transition once again.

2015 to 2029—Forty-Seven through Sixty-One Years Old

Supporting the Retired Baby Boom Cohort. One of the major problems facing your 1968 cohort in their late forties and fifties will be supporting the Baby Boom cohort as it moves out of the labor force and into retirement. This will be one time when being a member of a small cohort will be a disadvantage. As the Baby Boom cohort retires between 2010 and 2030, the proportion of people sixty-five and over in the population will greatly increase. Their retirement expectations will place heavier burdens on people younger than themselves than is presently the case.

Your 1968 cohort will be squeezed between the retired Baby Boom cohort's demands, and those of your own children and grandchildren. People younger than yourself can help you support the older population if birth rates rise and more potential workers are born between now and then (or if more young people immigrate into the nation—whether legally or illegally). This could mean solving the problem of supporting older people by adding an extra one hundred million younger people to the population.

But if birth rates continue to drop, it is possible to have more than fifty-eight people over sixty-five for every one hundred adults under sixty-five by the year 2050. If this happened, the Social Security system would be drastically altered. Retirement benefits probably would be reduced both for the Baby Boom and the Baby Bust retirees.

2030 and Later—Sixty-Two Years Old and Older

Retirement Expectations. Given the uncertainties about financing the retirement of the Baby Boom cohort, and what that could mean politically even before 2010, you may wish to reduce your dependency on the federal Social Security System in your later years by taking certain actions now, and in coming years. You may wish to see the Social Security retirement system as a possible supplement to your other sources of retirement income, and nothing more.

Judging from the situation of people currently over sixty-five, you should plan to have retirement income from your savings and from your investments. If you own your own home by then, you should include it as one of your investments. You may want to consider working for pay (whether as an employee or self-employed) into your seventies. Paid employment was the most valuable source of income for some older people in the early 1980s. In making your occupational choices in your twenties and thirties, you may also want to take into account the possibility of earning, or setting up, a pension for yourself.

Retirement planning is important for both genders because a large fraction of your life could well be spent in retirement. Assuming you celebrate your sixty-fifth birthday in 2033, you can expect to live an additional seventeen years if you are a man, and twenty-three years if you are a woman. You could expect to live even longer than that average figure if you do not smoke, if you watch your blood pressure, and if you wear seat belts when riding in a car. That means you can expect your retirement period to last at least into your early eighties if you are a man, and into your late eighties if you are a woman.

You may be financially self-sufficient in your retirement regardless of what happens to Social Security. But what if you are not? Then you would be dependent on others—either the government or your own relatives. If you never married, or if you married but never had any children, however, you would have few, if any, close relatives to turn to in case of need. In this way your marriage and parenthood choices of your late twenties and early thirties could have direct consequences on your retirement prospects in your sixties and later.

This is an especially consequential matter for women because they generally live much longer than do men, have lower rates of remarriage, and usually have smaller accumulated economic reserves in the form of savings, investments, and pension benefits. In 2040, for example, when the 1968 cohort will be seventy-two, the Social Security Administration is projecting that more than one-fifth of the women in that cohort will have been widowed and not remarried. What this means in personal terms is that retirement planning is particularly important for unmarried women, and for childless married women.

CONCLUSION

These fragments of the 1968 cohort's life script reveal underlying social expectations not only for them, but also for most other young adult residents of the United States. As I have said before, however, the scenario is not a forecast. Unanticipated social, economic, and political events no doubt will alter our future life prospects. The projections may never happen even though they are based on what appear today to be reasonable assumptions. Only time will tell how accurate the projections eventually will be. You can see for yourself how well the scenario matches reality by keeping this book and referring to it in the future.

The scenario's value is in showing you what is likely to happen, and what your options are. Your life will be like no other because you are unique in your personality, capabilities, desires, and experiences. Yet many of the problems and opportunities you will face will be similar to those that thousands of other people your age will be facing. You will make your choices at about the same age they will, and from the same range of available options.

I hope the knowledge presented in this book will help you make the right choices for the life you want to live. If the book helps you improve your life prospects, then my major goal in writing it will have been fulfilled.

Afterword

I would like to hear your reactions to this book. What parts do you find most useful? Do you have any suggestions for improvements?

I would especially enjoy hearing how the knowledge contained in the book helped you improve your life prospects. Whether now or five, ten, or more years from now, please feel free to write directly to me at the following address:

> Robert E. Kennedy, Jr.
> Author—*Life Choices*
> Holt, Rinehart and Winston
> 383 Madison Avenue
> New York, New York
> 10017

Glossary of Population Terms

Census—An official enumeration of an entire population. In the United States the federal government has conducted a census of the population every ten years since 1790.

Cohort—A group of people who have (or have had) the same experience at the same time. The Baby Boom birth cohort, all persons born between 1946 and 1964, is unusually large.

Demography—The study of characteristics of human populations including size, geographic distribution, and birth, death, and marriage rates.

Emigration—The departure of persons from one region to live in another. Few people emigrate from the United States.

Fertility—Births in a population. Fertility in the United States was higher after World War II than it was during the Great Depression of the 1930s.

Immigration—The arrival of persons to live in a region. Hundreds of thousands of people immigrate to the United States each year.

Migration—The change of a person's place of residence from one locality to another (no direction indicated). Millions of people in the United States migrate each year.

Mortality—Deaths in a population. Experts expect lower mortality in the future as people change their lifestyles.

Projection—A calculation of what may happen based on clearly stated assumptions. Experts project three different population sizes in the year 2000 for the United States, each based on a different set of assumptions.

Suggested Readings and References

READINGS FOR CHAPTER ONE: THINKING ABOUT YOUR FUTURE

On the Sociological Perspective:

Peter L. Berger. *Invitation to Sociology: A Humanistic Perspective.* Garden City, NY: Doubleday Anchor Books, 1963. A thoughtful presentation of what it is that sociologists do, and what is unique about the sociological perspective.

Ely Chinoy and John P. Hewitt. *Sociological Perspective*, 3d ed. New York: Random House, 1975. A straightforward and clearly written presentation of the fundamental concepts of sociology and the sociological perspective.

Stephen Cole. *The Sociological Orientation: An Introduction to Sociology*, 2d ed. Chicago: Rand McNally, 1979. Cole defines and illustrates the sociological perspective with examples from contemporary factual research.

Robert K. Merton. *Social Theory and Social Structure*, rev. ed. Glencoe, IL.: The Free Press, 1957. An advanced presentation of a structural approach to sociology that includes in Part II, "Studies in Social and Cultural Structure," an examination of how individuals react to social pressures.

C. Wright Mills. *The Sociological Imagination*. New York: Oxford University Press, 1959. An enduring classic that takes a pragmatic, critical approach to sociology.

David Riesman (with Nathan Glazer and Reuel Denney). *The Lonely Crowd: A Study of the Changing American Character*, abridged ed. New

Haven: Yale University Press, 1961. A classic description of tradition-directed, inner-directed, other-directed character types in the United States, and autonomy, adjustment, and anomie as personal behavior patterns.

Joseph A. Scimecca. *Society and Freedom: An Introduction to Humanist Sociology.* New York: St. Martin's Press, 1981. Scimecca believes that an impartial, dispassionate observation and analysis of society is not enough. He invites his readers to examine their own values and beliefs, and to test their ideas against reality.

Dennis H. Wrong. "The Oversocialized Conception of Man in Modern Sociology," *American Sociological Review*, Vol. 26, No. 2 (April 1961), pp. 183-193. Reprinted in Lewis A. Coser (ed.). *The Pleasures of Sociology.* New York: Mentor Books, 1980, pp. 8 - 25. Wrong argues that while people may be social creatures, they are never completely socialized.

On the Demographic Perspective:

Landon Y. Jones. *Great Expectations: America and the Baby Boom Generation.* New York: Ballantine Books, 1980. A blend of the cohort and life stages approaches that describes a particularly important birth cohort—the Baby Boom Babies, persons born from 1946 through 1964. Jones describes how the 76 million Americans born during this period are moving through their life stages.

Robert E. Kennedy, Jr. *The Irish: Emigration, Marriage, and Fertility.* Berkeley, CA: University of California Press, 1973. A combined sociological and demographic approach for understanding life choices in Ireland: why so many Irish left Ireland between 1841 and 1966; why those who remained married so late in life or never married at all; and how the large average family sizes in Ireland may have been caused by the extreme Irish emigration and marriage patterns.

Dennis H. Wrong. *Population and Society*, 4th ed. New York: Random House, 1977. A concise presentation of the demographic perspective as it applies to certain topics. Wrong is issue- and policy-oriented, and discusses society-wide demographic processes.

On the Life Course Perspective:

Felix M. Berardo (special ed.). *Middle and Late Life Transitions. The Annals of the American Academy of Political and Social Science*, Vol. 464 (November 1982). A collection of articles describing recent research about the impact of social and environmental factors on adult role transitions.

Robert H. Binstock and Ethel Shanas (eds.). *Handbook of Aging and the Social Sciences.* New York: Van Nostrand Reinhold Company, 1976. A standard reference work consisting of twenty-five chapters about adult aging and the aged from the perspective of various social sciences.

Zena Smith Blau. *Aging in a Changing Society*, 2d ed. New York: Franklin Watts, 1981. A sociological analysis of the adult aging process that examines the importance of ethnicity, educational attainment, work status, friendship groups, and marital status.

Daniel J. Levinson, et al. *The Seasons of a Man's Life*. New York: Ballantine Books, 1978. A popular adult development book about the aging stages of adult men in the United States. Levinson uses a social psychological approach to interpret interviews collected from men between 1968 and 1970.

Gail Sheehy:

1. *Passages: Predictable Crises of Adult Life.* New York: E. P. Dutton, 1976
2. *Pathfinders: Overcoming the Crises of Adult Life and Finding Your Own Path to Well Being.* New York: Bantam Books, 1981.

Two popularly written, best-selling books taking the adult development approach and advocating that individuals should take charge of their lives to turn life transitions from crises into opportunities.

READINGS FOR CHAPTER TWO: LIFE PROSPECTS AND COHORT SIZE

American Demographics. P.O. Box 68, Ithaca, New York 14850. A popularly written magazine that translates population information for businessmen and the general public.

Leon F. Bouvier. "America's Baby Boom Generation: The Fateful Bulge," *Population Bulletin*, Vol. 35, Number 1 (April 1980). A detailed discussion of the Baby Boom cohort—what caused it, and its impact on both the society and its own members. (Available from the Population Reference Bureau, Inc., 1337 Connecticut Ave. N.W., Washington, D.C. 20036.)

Andrew Hacker (ed.). *U/S: A Statistical Portrait of the American People.* New York: Viking Press, 1983. A useful and entertaining collection of facts about the United States that includes preliminary results from the 1980 census. Written in a clear and conversational style.

Barbara J. Holmes. *Reading, Science, & Mathematics Trends: A Closer Look.* National Assessment of Educational Progress, Education Commission of the States, Suite 700, 1860 Lincoln St., Denver, Colorado 80295. Holmes analyzes reasons for declines in scores on standardized tests taken by one million students in the United States during the 1970s.

Landon Y. Jones. *Great Expectations: America and the Baby Boom Generation.* New York: Ballantine Books, 1981. A description of the life course of the Baby Boom cohort.

Jane Newitt. "The (P)lucky Generation," *American Demographics*, Vol. 5, No. 1 (January 1983). A concise description of the demographic fortunes of persons born between 1920 and 1940.

Population Reference Bureau, 1337 Connecticut Ave., N.W., Washington, D.C. 20036. A nonprofit educational organization engaged in disseminating population information. Publications include *Intercom, Population Bulletin, World Population Data Sheet,* and *Interchange.* Special annual membership rates are available for students ($5.00) and educators ($10 for primary/secondary and $15 for college).

Gregory Spencer and John F. Long. "The New Census Bureau Projections," *American Demographics,* Vol. 5, No. 4 (April 1983). The statistician in charge of United States national population projections and the chief of the Population Projections Branch of the U.S. Census Bureau discuss the assumptions and implications of the 1982/1983 population projections.

Statistics Canada. *Population Projections for Canada and the Provinces: 1976-2001,* Ottawa, Canada, February 1979. A series of seven population projections based on different sets of assumptions about migration, fertility, and mortality.

United States Bureau of the Census. *Statistical Abstract of the United States: 1982-83,* 103d ed., Washington, D.C., 1982. The first place to look for statistics about the United States population. Available in most libraries, and for sale by the Superintendent of Documents, U.S. Government Printing Office, Washington, D.C. 20402.

————. *Current Population Reports.* "Projections of the Population of the United States: 1982 to 2050 (Advance Report)," Series P-25, No. 922 (October 1982).

READINGS FOR CHAPTER THREE: HOW MUCH FORMAL EDUCATION?

Karl L. Alexander and Thomas W. Reilly. "Estimating the Effects of Marriage Timing on Educational Attainment: Some Procedural Issues and Substantive Clarifications," *American Journal of Sociology,* Vol. 87, No. 1 (July 1981), pp. 143-156. The authors conclude that early marriage is an educational liability for women but not for men, and that women are more likely than men to make an either-or choice regarding education and marriage.

Randall K. Filer. "Sexual Differences in Earnings: The Role of Individual Personalities and Tastes," *Journal of Human Resources,* Vol. 18, No. 1 (Winter 1983), pp. 82-99. Using a unique data set developed from the personnel records of almost 4,000 persons, Filer examines the importance of personality factors (sociability, desire for dominance, restraint, etc.), and values (including the importance of income, family life, and time for recreation) for the gender gap in earnings. He concluded that gender differences in personality and values explain some of the gender gap in earnings among those without any college schooling, but not among those with some college.

Martin M. Frankel and Debra E. Gerald. *Projections of Education Statistics to 1988-89.* Washington, D.C.: National Center for Education Statistics, 1980. The source of the projected college enrollment rate of the 1968 cohort in 1988.

Dennis P. Hogan and Michele Pazul. "The Occupational and Earnings Returns to Education among Black Men in the North," *American Journal of Sociology,* Vol. 87, No. 4 (January 1982), pp. 905-920. An analysis of education, employment, and income among black men living in the North that takes into account whether one's origin and education was in the North or the South.

Robert L. Kaufman. "A Structural Decomposition of Black-White Earnings Differentials," *American Journal of Sociology,* Vol. 89, No. 3 (November 1983), pp. 585-611. A highly technical analysis of possible reasons for the earnings gap between white and black men based on the 1970 United States census, including racial differences in occupations. The author calculated that one-seventh of the earnings gap in 1969 between white and black men was caused by different occupational distributions.

Margaret Mooney Marini. "The Transition to Adulthood: Sex Differences in Educational Attainment and Age at Marriage," *American Sociological Review,* Vol. 43 (August 1978), pp. 483-507. An extensive, statistically based yet clearly written analysis of the association between educational attainment and several factors including gender, age at first marriage, grade-point average, and social status of parents. The most important factor limiting a woman's education was an early age at first marriage, while this was not the case among men.

Mary C. Regan and Helen Elizabeth Roland. "University Students: A Change in Expectations and Aspirations Over the Decade," *Sociology of Education,* Vol. 55 (October 1982), pp. 223-228. A concise description of the life goals of men and women students between 1952 and 1980 at the University of California, Davis, and at Cornell University. Interest in a career was increasing among women but decreasing among men. Interest in family was decreasing among both genders.

Rachel A. Rosenfeld. "Race and Sex Differences in Career Dynamics," *American Sociological Review,* Vol. 45, No. 4 (August, 1980), pp. 583-609. Rosenfeld uses information from large, national surveys asked each year over a period of six years of the same individuals. Besides race and sex, she also examined the influence on wages and status of one's education, initial job, and family background.

Joyce A. Stevens and Roger A. Herriot. "Current Earnings Differentials of Men and Women: Some Explanatory Regression Analyses," *American Statistical Association Proceedings of the Social Statistics Section (1975),* pp. 673-678. A technical analysis of the influence of breaks in lifetime employment on earnings. Both sexes experienced important reductions in earning power by leaving the labor force for two or more years.

Donald J. Treiman and Patricia A. Roos. "Sex and Earnings in Industrial Society: A Nine-Nation Comparison," *American Journal of Sociology*, Vol. 89, No. 3 (November 1983), pp. 612-650. A clearly written analysis of why women earn less than men among full-time workers in nine industrial nations including the United States. Extensive references to the literature on gender differences in income are included. The authors conclude that deeply entrenched social institutions and values limit women's opportunities and achievements.

U.S. Bureau of the Census. "Money Income of Household, Families, and Persons in the United States: 1981." *Current Population Reports*. Series P-60, No. 137 (March, 1983). The source of the 1981 income and earnings by gender, age, race, and work labor force status in 1982.

————. "Lifetime Earnings Estimates for Men and Women in the United States: 1979," *Current Population Reports*, Series P-60, No. 139 (February 1983). The source of estimates of lifetime earnings for persons born in 1961 by gender and labor force status. This report also presents lifetime earnings estimates from 1979 through age 64 for persons born in 1954, 1944, 1934, and 1924.

————. *Statistical Abstract of the United States: 1968*. 89th ed. Washington, D.C. 1968. The source of the fields of study among earned degrees conferred on men and women in 1966 (Table 199, page 135).

————. *Statistical Abstract of the United States: 1982-83*. 103d ed. Washington, D.C. 1982. The source of educational statistics including college graduates among whites, blacks, and Hispanics (Table 226, page 143), and earned degrees conferred in 1980 by field of study for men and women (Table 278, page 167).

READINGS FOR CHAPTER FOUR: WHICH OCCUPATION?

A. Regula Herzog. "High School Seniors' Occupational Plans and Values: Trends in Sex Differences 1976 through 1980," *Sociology of Education*, Vol. 55 (January 1982), pp. 1-13. Based on large national surveys of high-school seniors taken in the late 1970s and in 1980, Herzog found marked sex differences in work plans. Only a few sex differences in occupational plans were declining.

Joan Huber and Glenna Spitze. *Sex Stratification: Children, Housework, and Jobs*. New York: Academic Press, 1983. Huber and Spitze analyze information from a 1978 national sample to study the division of household labor, marital stability, and sex-role attitudes. They conclude that as women move into the labor force, men may become more involved in off-the-job private and family life.

Ronald C. Kessler and James A. McCrae, Jr. "The Effect of Wives' Employment on the Mental Health of Married Men and Women," *American Sociological Review*, Vol. 47, No. 2 (April 1982), pp. 216-227. Based on large national surveys, this report concludes that working outside the home improves a wife's mental health, while having an employed wife increases a husband's psychological distress.

Paul Lindsay and William E. Knox. "Continuity and Change in Work Values among Young Adults: A Longitudinal Study," *American Journal of Sociology*, Vol. 89, No. 4 (January 1984), pp. 918-931. A technical report using a sample of 9,208 high-school seniors that verifies: (1) the importance of work values for educational attainment and occupational choice; and (2) the preference of women for intrinsic job rewards, and of men for extrinsic rewards.

Lloyd B. Lueptow. "Sex-Typing and Change in the Occupational Choices of High School Seniors: 1964-1975," *Sociology of Education*, Vol. 54 (January 1981), pp. 16-24. A comparison of occupational plans and preferences of young adults revealed: (1) more women moving into traditionally male white-collar jobs; and (2) no meaningful change in the sex-typing of traditionally female jobs and of male skilled blue-collar jobs. In 1975 the majority still expected and hoped to enter occupations dominated by their own sex.

Gail M. Martin. "Math and Your Career," *Occupational Outlook Quarterly*, Vol. 27, No. 2 (Summer 1983), pp. 28-31. Martin presents a table showing how different levels of mathematics are used in one hundred occupations. She concludes that mathematics is becoming increasingly important in the working world.

————. and Melvin C. Fountain. "Matching Yourself with the World of Work," *Occupational Outlook Quarterly*, Vol. 26, No. 4 (Winter 1982), pp. 2-12. This report consists of a chart that defines sixteen occupational characteristics and requirements, and then lists all sixteen as they apply to over 250 occupations chosen from the 1982-83 *Occupational Outlook Handbook*.

Jeylan T. Mortimer and Jon Lorence. "Work Experience and Occupational Value Socialization: A Longitudinal Study," *American Journal of Sociology*, Vol. 84 (1979), pp. 1361-1385. This study documents the importance of values for making occupational choices, and of how working itself can change a person's occupational values.

Jon Sargent. "The Job Outlook for College Graduates during the 1980s," *Occupational Outlook Quarterly*, Vol. 26, No. 2, (Summer 1982), pp. 3-7. A concise and readable description of the reasons for, and the consequences of, the oversupply of college graduates during the 1970s and the 1980s. Sargent expects college graduates entering the labor force during the 1980s to exceed job openings by as many as three million.

Roberta G. Simmons and Dale A. Blyth. *Moving Into Adolescence: The Impact of Pubertal Change and School Context.* Forthcoming. Simmons and

Blyth report on changes between sixth and tenth grade in boys' and girls' attitudes about going to college, working as an adult, and (for girls) how having children would affect work attitudes.

U.S. Bureau of the Census. "Population Estimates and Projections," *Current Population Reports*, Series P-25, No. 922 (October 1982), p. 10. This report presents projections of the United States by age, sex, and race through 2050.

—————. *Statistical Abstract of the United States: 1982-83*, 103d ed. Washington, D.C. 1982.

U.S. Department of Labor. *Monthly Labor Review*. An important source of statistics, research, and commentary about the United States labor force both now and in the future.

—————. *Occupational Outlook Handbook*, 1982-83 ed. Washington, D.C.: Superintendent of Documents, April 1982. This reference book is the first place to look if you have questions about specific careers and jobs. It is written for the general public and updated regularly. The 1982-83 edition includes detailed information about 250 occupations—what the work is like, education required, job openings, and pay.

—————. *Occupational Projections and Training Data*, 1982 ed. Washington, D.C.: Superintendent of Documents, December 1982. Similar in format to the *Occupational Outlook Handbook*, but written in more technical language for an audience of education planners, training officials, and other professionals in the field. The 1982 edition includes projected employment in 1990, and percent change between 1980 and 1990, for 670 specific occupations employing 5,000 or more persons in 1980.

Mary Ellen Verheyden-Hilliard. "Girls Will Be Workers: Avoiding Yesterday's Stereotypes in Today's Career Education," *Occupational Outlook Quarterly*, Vol. 25, No. 3 (Fall 1981), pp. 16-21. An argument for educating young women about the probability that most will be employed at least until their fifties. Verheyden-Hilliard advocates career education in the primary grades and in high school designed to replace out-moded stereotypes with current facts about the employment of women.

Linda J. Waite. "U.S. Women at Work," *Population Bulletin*, Vol. 36, No. 2 (May 1981), pp. 1-43. A concise and well written summary of twentieth century trends in women's employment in the United States through 1980. Waite reports that the surge in women's employment since the 1950s was linked with: (1) improved education; (2) delayed marriage; (3) lower fertility; (4) more divorce and separation; (5) more openings in clerical and service jobs; (6) inflation; and (7) changed attitudes about sex roles.

Patrick D. Walsh. "Comparing Occupations: Four Measures," *Occupational Outlook Quarterly*, Vol. 26, No. 3 (Fall 1982), pp. 27-30. Walsh presents a chart comparing 177 occupations ranked according to their standings on four criteria—size, growth, earnings, and unemployment. He also lists the educational requirements of each occupation (high-school graduate only, some postsecondary training, or college graduate).

Work and Occupations: An International Sociological Journal. Beverly Hills, CA: Sage Publications. This journal specializes in sociological research analyzing the social context in which work occurs, and in the social meaning of occupations. The August, 1982 issue (Volume 9, Number 3), is devoted to articles about people who crossed the gender line on the job—including women autoworkers, women lawyers in England, and male strippers.

READINGS FOR CHAPTER FIVE: MARRIED OR UNMARRIED?

Jessie Bernard. *The Future of Marriage.* New Haven, CT: Yale University Press, 1982. Bernard describes changes during the 1970s in marriage and sex roles, and concludes that marriage is more beneficial for men than for women.

Philip Blumstein and Pepper Schwartz. *American Couples.* New York: William Morrow and Company, 1983. A popularly written report by two sociologists about couples (married couples as well as cohabitating heterosexuals and homosexuals), based on a survey of 6,000 couples taken in the late 1970s. The authors argue that the balance of power between the two partners strongly influences the couple's sexual activity, the provider role, handling money, and doing housework.

Andrew J. Cherlin. *Marriage, Divorce, Remarriage.* Cambridge, MA: Harvard University Press, 1981. A clearly written report covering historical and cohort trends in marital status in the United States. A separate chapter deals with black marriage patterns.

James Allan Davis. *General Social Surveys, 1972-1982; 1972-83.* Chicago: National Opinion Research Center, 1982, 1983. Includes questions about marriage, sex roles, and divorce. Distributed by the Roper Center, University of Connecticut, Storrs, Connecticut, 06268.

Joseph F. Faber and John C. Wilkin. "Social Security Area Population Projections, 1981," *Actuarial Study No. 85*, SSA Pub. No. 11-11532 (July 1981), Table 20, pp. 56-57. The source for the 1995 marital status projections presented in this chapter.

Noreen Goldman and Graham Lord. "Sex Differences in Life Cycle Measures of Widowhood," *Demography*, Vol. 20, No. 2 (May 1983), pp. 177-195. A technical analysis of widowhood studying the result of mortality and age differences between spouses at marriage. Data since 1950 are covered, as are racial differences.

Marcia Guttentag and Paul F. Secord. *Too Many Women? The Sex Ratio Question.* Beverly Hills, CA: Sage Publications, 1983. Two social psychologists argue that the sex ratio among unmarried people influences sexual behavior, marriage patterns, and the status of women generally. A shortage of women favors monogamy and restricts women to domestic roles. A surplus of women reduces the commitment of men to one woman for life, and increases the power of men over women.

Journal of Marriage and the Family. Published by the National Council on Family Relations, Fairview Community School Center, 1910 West County Road B, Suite 147, St. Paul, MN, 55113. Available in large public libraries and most universities, this journal is one of the major mediums for sociological research and theory related to marriage and the family.

George Masnick and Mary Jo Bane. *The Nation's Families: 1960-1990.* Boston, Mass.: Auburn House, 1980. A detailed description of marriage and divorce trends among cohorts between 1960 and 1975, with projections to 1990. Written to present policymakers with a brief summary of major changes in family life in the United States.

National Center for Health Statistics. "Advance Report of Final Divorce Statistics, 1980," *Monthly Vital Statistics Report,* Vol. 32, No. 3, Supplement (June 27, 1983). The source for recent facts about divorce rates by sex, age, and geographic region.

—————. "Advance Report of Final Marriage Statistics, 1980" *Monthly Vital Statistics Report,* Vol. 32, No. 5, Supplement (August 18, 1983). The source for recent facts about marriage and remarriage rates by sex, age, and geographic region.

Alexander A. Plateris, "Divorces by Marriage Cohort," *Vital and Health Statistics,* Series 21, Number 34 (August 1979). DHEW Publication No. (PHS) 79-1912. A technical study of divorce among marriage cohorts (all couples married during a given calendar year), covering marriages from 1922 through 1975.

Ira L. Reiss. "Some Observations on Ideology and Sexuality in America," *Journal of Marriage and the Family,* Vol. 43, No. 2 (May 1981), pp. 271-283. In this revised version of his Presidential Address to the National Council on Family Relations, Reiss describes the Traditional-Romantic and the Modern-Naturalistic sexual ideologies.

Robert B. Schafer and Patricia M. Keith. "Equity in Marital Roles across the Family Life Cycle," *Journal of Marriage and the Family,* Vol. 43, No. 2 (May 1981), pp. 359-367. In this study of fairness of marital roles, the authors report that wives perceived unfairness more frequently than did husbands.

Graham B. Spanier. "Married and Unmarried Cohabitation in the United States: 1980," *Journal of Marriage and the Family,* Vol. 45, No. 2 (May 1983), pp. 277 - 288. A study comparing married couples with unmarried couples in 1980 according to previous marital status, age, race, education, employment, and income.

U.S. Bureau of the Census, *Historical Statistics of the United States, Colonial Times to 1970.* Part 1. Washington, D.C., 1975. Series A-160-171, pages 20-21.

—————. "Marital Status and Living Arrangements: March 1980," *Current Population Reports,* Series P-20, No. 365 (October 1981).

—————. *Statistical Abstract of the United States: 1982-83,* 103d ed. Washington, D.C., 1982.

Linda J. Waite and Glenna D. Spitze. "Young Women's Transition to Marriage," *Demography*, Vol. 18, No. 4 (November 1981), pp. 681-694. An analysis of yearly interviews conducted between 1968 and 1973 of 5,000 young women. The major question was whether a young woman's parental family background affects her chances of marrying before age eighteen.

James A. Weed. "Divorce: American's Style," *American Demographics*, Vol. 4, No. 3 (March 1982), pp. 13-17. A nontechnical report detailing recent trends in divorce in the United States, how long current marriages can be expected to last, and speculations about future divorce rates.

READINGS FOR CHAPTER SIX: CHILDFREE OR PARENT?

Joan Aldous. *Family Careers: Developmental Change in Families*. New York: John Wiley & Sons, 1978. A well-organized and clearly written description of changes in families from their formation through their dissolution. The author, a family sociologist, uses the family life cycle as a means for analyzing relationships between husbands and wives, parents and children, and among siblings.

Thomas K. Burch (ed.). *Demographic Behavior: Interdisciplinary Perspectives on Decision-Making*. Boulder, CO: Westview, 1980. A collection of essays by sociologists, economists, psychologists, and demographers that attempts to explain why people have children.

James Allan Davis. *General Social Surveys, 1972-1982*. Chicago: National Opinion Research Center, 1982. Tabulations of the responses to questions covering a wide range of topics asked each year in national public opinion surveys. Questions about family life, children, and birth control usually are included. Distributed by the Roper Center, University of Connecticut, Storrs, Connecticut, 06268.

Family Planning Perspectives. A bimonthly journal published by the Alan Guttmacher Institute, 360 Park Avenue South, New York, N. Y., 10010. Written for professionals working in the field of family planning, this journal provides up-to-date information about contraceptive methods and abortion including usage, public policies, public opinions, and technological changes.

Jacqueline Darroch Forrest and Stanley K. Henshaw. "What U.S. Women Think and Do About Contraception," *Family Planning Perspectives*, Vol. 15, No. 4 (July/August 1983), pp. 157-166. Based on a 1982 survey of 10,000 women, Forrest and Henshaw report on attitudes about contraception and abortion, and on age patterns of contraceptive use.

Gerry E. Hendershot and Paul J. Placek (eds.). *Predicting Fertility*. Lexington, MA: D.C. Heath, Lexington Books, 1981. Articles commenting on the uses and shortcomings of surveys asking people about their childbearing plans.

Lois W. Hoffman and Martin L. Hoffman. "The Value of Children to Parents," in James T. Fawcett (ed.), *Psychological Perspectives on Population*.

New York: Basic Books, 1973, pp. 19-76. An analytic review of the socio-logical and psychological literature concerning the value people in various cultures and times have placed on having children.

Sheila B. Kamerman. *Parenting in an Unresponsive Society: Managing Work and Family.* New York: The Free Press, 1980. A report on the ways in which working mothers cope with the demands made upon them by their job and family responsibilities. Based on the results of interviews with 205 working mothers.

William D. Mosher. "Fertility and Family Planning in the 1970s: The National Survey of Family Growth," *Family Planning Perspectives,* Vol. 14, No. 6 (November/December 1982), pp. 314-320. Mosher, a demographic statistician, summarizes the major findings of national fertility surveys done in the mid-1970s. He gives particular attention to racial differences in fertility and birth control usage.

National Survey of Family Growth. See William D. Mosher's summary cited above.

Anne R. Pebley and David E. Bloom. "Childless Americans," *American Demographics,* Vol. 4, No.1 (January 1982), pp. 18-21. A summary of recent and possible future trends in childlessness in the United States. The authors report that the voluntarily childless woman is typically white, urban, highly educated, employed, and more likely to be divorced or separated. Bloom projects that over thirty percent of white women born in 1954 could remain childless, as well as more than eighteen percent of black women born in the same year.

Cheryl Russell. "Who's Having Those Babies?" *American Demographics,* Vol. 4, No.1 (January 1982), pp. 36-38. A brief, nontechnical summary of major social characteristics associated with childbearing including age, race, education, and labor force status. Based on the June, 1980 Current Population Survey conducted by the Census Bureau.

Gregory Spencer and John F. Long. "The New Census Bureau Projections," *American Demographics,* Vol. 5, No. 4 (April 1983), pp. 24-31. An expert discussion of the assumptions and implications of the 1982/83 United States population projections.

U.S. Bureau of the Census. "Projections of Number of Households and Families, 1979 to 1995," *Current Population Reports,* Series P-25, No. 805 (1979). The source of projections used in this chapter of married couple, other family, and nonfamily households in 1995.

—————. "Projections of the Population of the United States: 1982 to 2050 (Advance Report)," *Current Population Reports,* Series P-25, No. 922 (October 1982). The source of projections to 2050 of the total population size of the United States under high, middle, or low fertility assumptions.

—————. "Projections of the Population of the United States by Age, Sex, and Race: 1983 to 2080," *Current Population Reports,* Series P-25, No. 952 (May 1984). The most recent national population projections available at the time of this writing.

————. "Marital Status and Living Arrangements: March 1980," *Current Population Reports*, Series P-20, No. 365 (October 1981).

————. "Fertility of American Women: June 1982." *Current Population Reports*, Series P-20, No. 379 (May 1983).

————. *Statistical Abstract of the United States: 1982-83*, 103d ed. Washington, D.C., 1982.

————. *Historical Statistics of the United States, Colonial Times to 1970*, Part 1. Washington, D.C., 1975. Series A-160-171, pp. 20-21.

Jean E. Veevers. *Childless by Choice*. Toronto: Butterworths, 1980. Based on interviews with 156 childless persons, Veevers examines such concerns as deciding to be childless, resisting pressures for having children, and policies encouraging people to have children.

Stephanie J. Ventura. "Births of Hispanic Parentage, 1980," *National Center for Health Statistics Monthly Vital Statistics Report*, Vol. 32, No. 6 Supplement (September 1983). A detailed summary of Hispanic fertility in 1980 by race, marital status, educational attainment, prenatal care, and birth weight.

READINGS FOR CHAPTER SEVEN: HOMEOWNER OR RENTER? MOVER OR STAYER?

Felix M. Berardo (ed.). *Middle and Late Life Transitions*. Beverly Hills, CA: Sage Publications. This is a special issue of *The Annals* of the American Academy of Political and Social Science, Vol. 464 (November 1982). It is a collection of research reports about middle age and aging that emphasize role transitions—such as the empty nest period after children have left the household, retirement from the labor force, or living alone after being widowed.

Suzanne M. Bianchi, Reynolds Farley, and Daphne Spain. "Racial Inequalities in Housing: An Examination of Recent Trends," *Demography*, Vol. 19, No. 1 (February 1982), pp. 37-51. A review of changes in the housing situations (both homeownership and housing quality) of whites and blacks between 1960 and 1977. Although blacks were less likely to be homeowners, and were more likely to live in lower-quality housing, the differences were much smaller in 1977 than seventeen years earlier.

John C. Henretta. "Parental Status and Child's Home Ownership," *American Sociological Review*, Vol. 49, No. 1 (February 1984), pp. 131-140. A technical analysis of the relation between parents' social status and their children's homeownership using a national sample taken in 1980 of 1,623 whites and 1,215 blacks. Henretta concluded that parents' income had no effect on the likelihood of children becoming homeowners.

Thomas C. Marcin. "Population Change as Related to Long-Term Cycles in Residential Construction in the United States," *Forest Products Laboratory Research Paper FPL 392*, U. S. Department of Agriculture, Forest Service, (March 1981). A technical analysis of the effects of changing cohort sizes on potential housing demand in the United States to 2030.

Angela M. O'Rand and John C. Henretta. "Women at Middle Age: Developmental Transitions," in F. M. Berardo (ed.), *Middle and Late Life Transitions.* Beverly Hills, CA: Sage Publications, 1982, pp. 57-64. Sociologists O'Rand and Henretta describe how midlife transitions for women are related to earlier decisions about marriage, childbearing, and paid employment. Low fertility completed early in life, for example, leads in midlife to an extended empty nest period and an increased likelihood of labor force participation.

Gary D. Sandefur and Wilbur J. Scott. "A Dynamic Analysis of Migration: An Assessment of the Effects of Age, Family and Career Variables," *Demography*, Vol. 18, No. 3 (August 1981), pp. 355-368. This technical analysis of the migration histories of men in their thirties concludes that the decline in mobility with increasing age is due almost entirely to commitments to family and employment.

George Sternlieb and James W. Hughes. "The Coming Housing Bust," *American Demographics*, Vol. 4, No. 10 (November 1982), pp. 32-33. The authors argue that the high homeownership rates of the late 1970s were made possible by unusually favorable conditions for home mortgages. As home financing costs rise during the 1980s, the authors project smaller housing units being built, and a decline in the number of new units constructed.

————. "Who's Buying Homes?" *American Demographics*, Vol. 4, No. 11 (December 1982), pp. 24-26. A report on the characteristics of people who bought homes in 1980, including whether married couples were childless or had dependents.

————. "The Housing Locomotive and the Demographic Caboose," *American Demographics*, Vol. 6, No. 3 (March 1984), pp. 22-27. The authors point out that household formation depends on housing availability. If housing is not available or affordable, then people will either make greater use of existing accommodations or choose not to form separate households.

Lois M. Tamir. "Men at Middle Age: Developmental Transitions," in F. M. Berardo (ed.), *Middle and Late Life Transitions*. Beverly Hills, CA: Sage Publications, 1982, pp. 47-56. Social-psychologist Tamir describes how middle-aged men adjust to changes in their work roles, their family life, and relations with friends and community. She suggests a trade-off occurs with work becoming less central to their lives, and family and social relationships becoming more so.

Kenneth R. Tremblay, Jr. and Don A. Dillman. *Beyond the American Housing Dream: Accommodation to the 1980s.* New York: University Press of America, 1983. An excellent introduction to the sociology of housing that not only reviews the research on housing done by sociologists, but also presents the results of a survey of housing preferences and values among 2,800 households in Washington state in 1977.

U. S. Bureau of the Census. *1980 Census of Housing*, Vol. 4, "Components of Inventory Change: United States and Regions, Characteristics of Housing Units," HC80-4-1 (August 1983), 597 pages plus appendices. This 1980 census publication is the source of detailed information about homeowners and renters by age, gender, marital status, race, Spanish origin, children living in the household, education of householder, and region.

―――――. "Geographic Mobility: March 1981 to March 1982," *Current Population Reports* Series P-20, No. 384 (February 1984). The primary source used in this chapter for facts about which people were movers and which were settled down. The report is based on a national survey of 58,000 households taken in March, 1982.

―――――. "Estimates of the Population of the United States, by Age, Sex, and Race: 1980 to 1983," *Current Population Reports* Series P-25, No. 949 (May 1984). This report presents details by age, gender, and race about the sizes of single-year birth cohorts in 1983.

―――――. *Statistical Abstract of the United States: 1982-83*, 103d ed. Washington, D.C. The source of such information through 1981 about housing as the: (1) proportions of homeowners among all householders in the fifty states and in some large cities; (2) average age of first-home buyers; and (3) prices paid and downpayments made by first-home buyers.

―――――. *Statistical Abstract of the United States: 1984*, 104th ed. Washington, D.C. Similar housing data is updated through 1982, as well as serving as the source for information about state differences in residential mobility.

READINGS FOR CHAPTER EIGHT: WHAT CAN YOU EXPECT IN RETIREMENT?

Robert C. Atchley. "Retirement: Leaving the World of Work," in F. M. Berardo (ed.), *Middle and Late Life Transitions.* Beverly Hills, CA: Sage Publications, 1982, pp. 120-130. A concise description of the process of retirement from attitudes about retirement, through retirement policies, to factors in the decision to retire. Atchley concludes that most retired people with secure incomes and adequate health adjust well to retirement.

Harry C. Ballantyne. "Actuarial Status of the OASI and DI Trust Funds," *Social Security Bulletin,* Vol. 47, No. 5 (May 1984), pp. 3-8. The Chief Actuary of the Social Security Administration provides a clearly written and well-illustrated summary of the 1984 Annual Report of the Board of Trustees of the Federal Old-Age and Survivors Insurance (OASI) and Disability Insurance (DI) Trust Funds.

Joseph F. Faber and Alice H. Wade. "Life Tables for the United States: 1900-2050," *Actuarial Study No. 89* (December 1983), Office of the Actuary, Social Security Administration, SSA Pub. No. 11-11536.This report lists average life expectancies for the United States from 1900 through 1980, and projects life expectancies through 2050. It also includes the life expectancies of specific birth cohorts on reaching certain ages.

Sol Mussey. "Actuarial Status of the HI and SMI Trust Funds," *Social Security Bulletin*, Vol. 47, No. 5 (May, 1984), pp. 9-16. The Director of the Division of Medicare Cost Estimates, Health Care Financing Administration, summarizes the 1984 annual report of the Medicare Board of Trustees. The Medicare Board is concerned about the rising costs of Medicare, and recommends to Congress that ways be found to curtail future program costs.

National Association of Mature People. *A Retirement Planning Guide.* Oklahoma City, OK, 1984. Considered by some to be the best one-volume retirement planning guide. Although intended for middle-income, middle-aged people, it also provides young adults with a valuable preview of the practical side of planning for retirement. Copies may be obtained from NAMP, P.O. Box 26792, Oklahoma City, OK, 73126.

Fred C. Pampel and Jane A. Weiss. "Economic Development, Pension Policies, and Labor Force Participation of Aged Males: A Cross-national, Longitudinal Approach," *American Journal of Sociology*, Vol. 89, No. 2 (September, 1983), pp. 350-372. A technical analysis of the reasons why older men increasingly withdrew from the labor force in eighteen countries between 1950 and 1975.

Lois B. Shaw. "Retirement Plans of Middle-Aged Married Women," *The Gerontologist*, Vol. 24, No. 2 (1984), pp. 154-158. Based on the responses of over 800 working wives, Shaw concludes that most do not plan to retire at the same time as their husbands. Women's retirement plans are strongly influenced by their own eligibility for a pension and for Social Security.

Jacob S. Siegel. "On the Demography of Aging," *Demography*, Vol. 17, No. 4 (November 1980), pp. 345-364. An excellent review of demographic research published in the 1970s and 1980 concerning such topics as the age compositions of populations, prospects for greater longevity, the life course, retirement, and Social Security policies.

Social Security Bulletin. This journal is written for members of the general public who are interested in the current status and policies of the various Social Security programs. An official publication of the Social Security Administration, it is available through most large public libraries, many college and university libraries, or by subscription directly from the Superintendent of Documents, U.S. Government Printing Office, Washington, D.C. 20402.

Judith Treas and Vern L. Bengston. "The Demography of Mid- and Late-Life Transitions," in F. M. Berardo (ed.), *Middle and Late Life Transitions.* Beverly Hills, CA: Sage Publications, 1982, pp. 11-21. A clearly written description of how the increase in life expectancies during the past eighty years has been linked to the length of time married couples spend together after their children have left home, retirement, and living alone late in life.

John Trout and David R. Mattson. "A Ten-Year Review of the Supplemental Security Income Program," *Social Security Bulletin*, Vol. 47, No. 1 (January 1984). A review of the first ten years of this federal program for the needy aged, blind, and disabled that compares its performance with its original goals and expectations.

United States Bureau of the Census. "Money Income of Households, Families, and Persons in the United States, 1982," *Current Population Reports*, Series P-60, No. 142 (February 1984). Each year the government asks several thousand households how much income they had the previous year. The facts presented in this report are based on a national survey of 59,000 households interviewed in March, 1982.

United States Social Security Administration. *1984 Annual Report of the Board of Trustees of the Federal Old-Age and Survivors Insurance and Disability Insurance Trust Funds.* Washington, D.C.: U.S. Government Printing Office, April 5, 1984. The Trustees of Social Security are the Secretaries of the Treasury, of Labor, and of Health and Human Services in addition to the Commissioner of Social Security. Each year they report to Congress on the current and long-term financial soundness of the system. To obtain your free copy of their most recent report, write to: Office of Public Inquiries, Room 4100 Annex, Social Security Administration, 6401 Security Boulevard, Baltimore, Maryland 21235.

John C. Wilkin. "Social Security Area Population Projections, 1983," *Actuarial Study No. 88*, (August 1983), Social Security Administration, SSA Pub. No. 11-11535. Wilkin summarizes the population projections through 2080 by age, sex, and marital status for the Social Security Area. Included in this population are the residents of the fifty states and the District of Columbia, armed forces overseas, other citizens overseas, and the civilian residents of Puerto Rico, the Virgin Islands, Guam, and American Samoa.

READINGS FOR CHAPTER NINE: MAKING CHOICES IN AN AGE OF UNCERTAINTY

Peter L. Berger. *Invitation to Sociology: A Humanistic Perspective.* Garden City, N.Y.: Doubleday Anchor Books, 1963. The relationship between "determinism" (cultural) and "free will" (personal choice) is well set forth in Chapters Four and Five: "Sociological Perspective—Man in Society," and "Sociological Perspective—Society in Man."

Harrison Brown. *The Human Future Revisited: The World Predicament and Possible Solutions.* New York: W.W. Norton, 1978. One of the best summaries of the links between world population growth, the growing gap between rich and poor nations, food and energy constraints, and the risk of thermonuclear war.

William R. Catton, Jr. *Overshoot: The Ecological Basis of Revolutionary Change.* Urbana, IL: University of Illinois Press, 1982. A human ecologist's view of the environmental limits to the growth in the numbers, and in the living standards, of the world population. Catton argues against the belief that technology will save us, and for the acceptance of a sense of limits and moderation.

Sar A. Levitan and Clifford M. Johnson. "The Future of Work: Does It Belong to Us or to the Robots?" *Monthly Labor Review*, Vol. 105, No. 9 (September 1982), pp. 10-14. The authors argue that the automation of factory, office, and some engineering and designing occupations will be more evolutionary than revolutionary during the 1990s. Investment constraints and the attitudes of both workers and consumers will slow the adoption of automated technologies.

John Naisbitt. *Megatrends: Ten New Directions Transforming Our Lives.* New York: Warner Books, 1982. In addition to the shift from an industrial to an information society, Naisbitt describes nine other transformations altering our futures. Several will increase your power of choice including trends toward decentralization, participatory democracy, greater self-reliance, and the decline of formal hierarchies with the rise of the less formal process of networking.

Alvin Toffler. *The Third Wave.* New York: Bantam Books, 1981. A popularly written and extensively documented description of the advent of societies based on information (the Third Wave) instead of the manufacture of material objects (the Second Wave), or the production of food and other basic commodities (the First Wave). Toffler argues that the new technologies and accompanying social values can reduce the risk of nuclear annihilation or ecological disaster.

The World Bank. *World Development Report 1984.* New York: Oxford University Press. The World Bank's annual report for 1984 examines the links between population change and economic development. It concludes that unless population growth is slowed, millions of people in the poorest countries, and the poorest groups in many other countries, can expect an even lower quality of life in the future.

Index